VIBRANT
PUNCH NEEDLE
DÉCOR

VIBRANT
PUNCH NEEDLE
DÉCOR

adorn your home
with colorful florals
& geometric patterns

Melissa Lowry

author of *Handmade Animal Dolls*

PAGE STREET
PUBLISHING CO.

PAGE STREET
PUBLISHING CO.

First published in 2020 by
Page Street Publishing Co.
27 Congress Street, Suite 105
Salem, MA 01970
www.pagestreetpublishing.com

Distributed by Macmillan, sales in Canada by The Canadian Manda Group.

24   23   22   21   20   1   2   3   4   5

ISBN-13: 978-1-64567-011-7
ISBN-10: 1-64567-011-2

Library of Congress Control Number: 2019951561

Cover and book design by Melissa Lowry
Photography by Melissa Lowry

Printed and bound in China

To my parents, for never letting me forget who I am and where I come from. For teaching me that my roots and customs are to be cherished regardless of where I live in the world. For pushing me to reach for my dreams. For their support and their love.

TABLE OF CONTENTS

INTRODUCTION

As a graphic designer who has always been fascinated with crafts, I found from a very early age that I needed to translate my designs into something tangible. Drawing and painting were always my media of choice, but I had a craving to turn my art into something more.

Learning how to embroider was the first craft I ever tackled growing up in Mexico. I remember my grandma showing me exquisite tablecloths and napkins embroidered either by her or a friend. I remember asking my mom to teach me: Without fabric or a hoop to practice on, I learned how to embroider on a piece of paper first. I'd draw a simple flower and embroider it. I got hooked immediately and asked for the proper materials to make my first napkin. Ever since then, I have had such admiration for the artisans who hand embroider and weave all the beautiful dresses, rugs, tablecloths and other textiles that were part of my daily life.

When I found the punch needle technique on social media, I knew I had to try it. Its resemblance to embroidery caught my eye. Working with the punch needle made the process fast and the results were beautiful. The needle allows you to pierce through fabric, making a loop on the underside effortlessly. Very few materials are needed to get started and the projects take shape quickly. It's portable and easy on your hands—what's not to love!

When I first saw it, my brain instantly filled with possibilities. I love that my designs can be translated easily to this technique. It also allows me to create big pieces a lot quicker; in a matter of minutes, I'm able to cover a large area and see the results immediately. It also gives me the option of choosing between the two finished sides, making the pieces reversible.

Best of all, punch needle allows you to experiment with materials. Feel free to use anything from leftover yarn, ribbon, floss or even fabric scraps. Look around you and see what you can use: perhaps you have an old cotton shirt you can cut into strips and recycle. If it fits through the needle and runs loosely through it, you can use it! It's up to you to create a piece that you're proud to display.

If you are new to punch needle, the Monarca butterfly project (page 45) is a great place to start. I don't think I've ever encountered a craft that is as simple and as forgiving as punch needle, so don't be afraid to make mistakes. They are easily fixed—that's the beauty of punch needle. If you've already picked up punch needle, there's a good chance you love it. I find it incredibly addicting because the results are immediate. The sound of that needle piercing through the fabric is almost therapeutic, and you can do it almost anywhere. It's a craft that has your head exploding with ideas of what you can do with it.

One of the things I want to emphasize is that you should not feel limited to any specific surface or material. If you can think it, then chances are you can make it—especially if you have sewing skills. You can also adapt the patterns in this book to meet your needs. If you think the Talavera Pillow (page 51) would look fabulous as a wall hanging in your bedroom, go for it!

The patterns and color palettes you see here are specific to my own style and influence. Feel free to change it up. Pick a palette that you already have going in your home. If you're feeling bold, give it a shot—every room needs a statement piece. There are also many geometric patterns and styles that you can draw inspiration from if you feel up to creating your own. The idea behind this book is that eventually you will become adventurous enough to design your own patterns.

My biggest hope is that my personal style and Mexican influence is reflected through these projects. Mexican textiles date back to pre-Hispanic times when indigenous women hand-dyed fibers and wove them into specific styles and patterns native to their region. Growing up, I remember taking for granted the beauty that surrounded me. Now as an adult, I refer back to those images that linger in my head for inspiration. The symbolism in Mexican culture is extensive, and there is so much to draw from. I encourage you to do a little research. I promise you'll be inspired by the many, many styles and colors of Mexican textiles.

I'm from Monterrey, which is in the northern part of the country. I traveled to Mexico City specifically for this book because I wanted to experience firsthand the huge artisan markets that characterize Mexico City and I wanted to meet and talk to the artisans who protect and preserve their craft. Many of the handicrafts are imported from nearby cities known for their handcrafted techniques and styles. You'll notice that each of the projects in this book is inspired by some of my memories and experiences there.

Whether you are learning to use the punch needle for the first time or you are looking for inspiration to continue your punching journey, I hope that you embrace the possibilities that this wonderful medium gives you. There is so much you can do, and this book only scratches the surface. Happy punching!

Melissa Lowry

GETTING STARTED

Punch needle is a relatively simple craft to pick up. There are really no complicated stitches, and you only need a few basic materials to get started. All you need is a punch needle, cloth, a frame, a fiber to punch with and an idea. And you don't have to stick to rugs or pillows. The possibilities are endless!

The punch needle does all the work for you—as you pierce the fabric, a loop is created on the other side. You decide how long the loop is by choosing the size of your needle: the longer the needle, the bigger the loops. As you punch, the series of loops you create will give you a unique and intricate piece.

Once you get the hang of how the punch needle works, you'll find yourself looking for surfaces to cover. It's a simple craft that you can take anywhere, which makes it accessible to those who only have a little time to dedicate to a project. A couple of minutes here and there will add up to a wonderful piece. Here are a few tips that I've learned along the way that have made my punching a little easier.

TOOLS & MATERIALS

PUNCH NEEDLES

In this book, I use two kinds of needles: One is an embroidery punch needle and the other is a rug hooking punch needle. Both work the same way, but they use different materials and work on different surfaces and achieve different looks. For the embroidery technique, I use the Ultra Punch® needle. An embroidery punch needle can be used for smaller, detailed projects, and it needs to be sealed on the back (see page 123). For the rug hooking technique, I use the Oxford punch needle. A rug hooking punch needle will cover a larger area quicker. It can be used with materials that will survive rough wear and tear, and it gives you a piece that is finished on both sides.

The look of your piece can vary depending on the size of the needle you use. You can mix and match sizes to add texture to your piece. The Ultra Punch needle comes with three different needle widths, and you can adjust the length of the needle by setting the number on the handle. Amy Oxford needles are sold separately in different sizes and widths. The longer the needle, the longer the loops it makes and the more yarn it uses. The widths correspond to the thickness of the yarn that it takes.

Different size needles will give you different textures.

Always keep the needle opening facing the direction you are punching in and the tip in contact with the cloth as you pull it to start your next stitch. If you pull it too far you will also pull out your stitch. If you find that your stitches are still coming out, you are likely not pressing the needle down as far as the handle can go or you could have some tension in your yarn that is pulling the stitch out.

Tip: When you're ready to venture out and create your own projects, make sure to decide which needle will work best before you get started.

YARN

There is a huge variety of yarn available out there and it can easily get overwhelming. What I like to do is begin by looking at the project I want to make. Does it go on the wall? Will it be used in a high traffic area? Will it get lots of wear? These will give you an idea of what yarn to look for. The projects in this book give suggestions for the best yarn to use.

A rug hooking punch needle uses thicker fibers such as yarn, fabric scraps or jute. It can only pierce loose-weave fabrics such as linen or monk's cloth. Rugs and larger pieces are done using the rug hooking punch needle as it uses materials that withstand use. It is much quicker to punch with. If you're working on a project that will get lots of

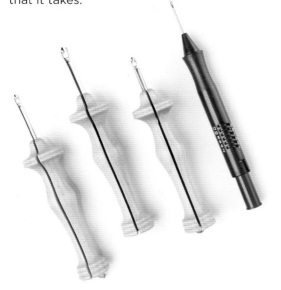

Experiment with different types of yarn. If they fit through your needle freely, use them!

Linen and monk's cloth are my favorite fabrics to use.

wear, a good rule of thumb is to go straight for the rug hooking yarn or wool yarn. Wool is known for its durability and strength to withstand wear and tear. You can even wash some of them on a delicate cycle. I've also used acrylic yarn in some projects, such as pillows, with great success.

An embroidery punch needle is used to get smaller, more detailed stiches. You can use embroidery floss, thin yarn or ribbon with it. The needle is super sharp and it pierces through most tight-weave fabrics, making it ideal for embellishing clothing or achieving fine detail work.

Think outside the box when it comes to materials. If you can feed it through the needle loosely—so it doesn't jam as you punch—you can use it!

Tip: Punching can go much quicker if you're not fighting with your yarn. I recommend balling your yarn before you start and having a yarn bowl handy. If you don't have a yarn bowl, any bowl will do. It will help prevent the yarn from rolling around, getting tangled or dirty.

BACKING FABRIC

When using the Oxford needle, my preferred material is a cotton 13 thread count monk's cloth. It's soft and forgiving. If you need to take out stitches, you can "heal" the holes by rubbing the needle or your nail over the cloth to make them disappear. Linen is another great fabric to punch on. There are different types of linen. For the projects in this book, I used natural linen because I like the tight weave for leaving the background unfinished. You can also get primitive linen, which has an evenly spaced weave of 12 × 12 threads per inch (2.5 cm), for larger projects that you wish to punch completely.

When using the embroidery punch needle, you can use almost anything with a tight weave. The test is to be sure that the thread stays as you pull out the needle. If it does, you are good to use it.

Your backing cloth needs to be big enough for the type of frame you choose. Make sure you cut more than you think you need; you need to be able to stretch it properly. There is nothing worse than being short and having to possibly waste that cloth. If your backing is too loose, you'll run into issues when punching. Always make sure it's taut!

STRETCHER FRAMES

There are a number of frames you can use depending on the size of your piece. To keep your project within budget—yarn can be expensive!—I recommend making your own frame. The easiest and most inexpensive way to do it if you don't have any carpentry skills is to buy canvas stretcher bars. You can get these in multiple sizes; be sure to measure the inside opening when calculating the size for your project. Simply staple the material to the frame and punch away. If you don't want to bother stapling your material every single time, you can attach carpet strips to the frame. These strips are very inexpensive and have nails that will keep the cloth taut until you take it off—perfect to keep reusing the frame without having to staple.

There are also premade stretcher frames available that come with gripper strips around the edges. These are fantastic for getting a properly stretched cloth every single time. You can also buy the gripper strips separately to attach to a frame that you've built on your own or recycled.

When using the embroidery punch needle, you are typically working on a smaller piece. A no-slip Morgan hoop works great, especially when adding a fun touch to clothing. A Q-Snap frame made from PVC tubing also does wonders when working with square or corner pieces. It allows you to adjust the tension with ease. Q-Snap frames are also buildable, and you can use them for small- to medium-sized rug hooking pieces as well.

I used four types of frames for the projects in this book:
- 30 × 20–inch (76.2 × 50.8–cm) wooden frame with carpet strips that I made
- 18 × 18–inch (45.7 × 45.7–cm) gripper frame from Amy Oxford
- 12-inch (30.5-cm) no-slip Morgan hoop
- 11 × 17–inch (27.9 × 43.2–cm) Q-Snap frame

If you don't have access to an Amy Oxford gripper frame, a regular canvas stretcher frame will do the trick.

Having these frames handy will allow you to make any of the projects in this book with the exception of the Flor Hanging Hoop (page 25) and the Campo Hanging Hoop (page 29), which are finished directly on the hoop.

The measurements I give for each project are for the punched area. You will need extra backing fabric to wrap around your frame. If you are stapling to the back of your frame, you'll need more than if you were using a frame with gripper strips.

For the rug hooking frames, it's really important to cover the gripper strips and carpet nails so that you don't injure yourself. Amy Oxford sells a frame cover, or if you're handy with a sewing machine, you can make one yourself. For the carpet strips, I use pool noodles that I purchased at the dollar store. Simply make a slit on one side and slip it on—works like a charm!

TEMPLATES & TRACING

The templates are my favorite part of this book. You can find them in the envelope inside the back cover. They are to scale and ready for you to use! No need to worry about printing and piecing them together; though, should you need to you can find them on my website at www.melissalowry.com/vibranttemplates

Always stretch your fabric first before you trace. If you don't, the design might warp when you are stretching it. If I'm being honest, I freehand my designs most of the time, but I will trace it when I want the design perfectly symmetrical and aligned. The method that has worked the best for me is transferring the design using carbon paper, but I will only use it when I plan to use the rug hooking punch needle as the lines will be hidden. If I'm working on a design that requires the whole piece to be punched and the marks will be covered, I won't hesitate to use a permanent marker or something that is more obvious.

For pieces that use the smaller embroidery punch needle, I use a heat transfer pen that gives me thinner lines or I trace the design against a window—tape the design on to a window and the fabric on top—using a water-soluble pen or pencil.

If a piece requires you to punch from the front and the back, assess how much punching will be required from the reverse. If it's a lot, trace it against the light. If it's a little, outline the shape first from the front and then flip it to punch the rest from the back. The initial outline made from the front gives you a guide as to what needs to be punched on the reverse. The tighter your stitches are on the front, the clearer your outline will be on the back. You will see me use this technique with some projects: the Barro Plant Pot (page 115) is a great example.

SCISSORS

I use fabric scissors, but you can get scissors that have a bent handle that make cutting yarn so much easier. Make sure that whatever scissors you use are sharp! This will prevent you from pulling the yarn and possibly undoing some stitches.

HOW TO PUNCH

If you've never tried punch needle before, you might be wondering how it all works and how it stays together. Don't worry! I'm confident you'll get the hang of it fairly quickly. Here are some basics to get you well on your way with both types of needles.

Grab the yarn or embroidery floss that fits your needle. Make sure it flows freely through the hole or the stitch won't hold.

On the Oxford needle, run the yarn through the handle slot down to the needle. The slot should be facing forward toward the direction you are punching in and the tail toward the back.

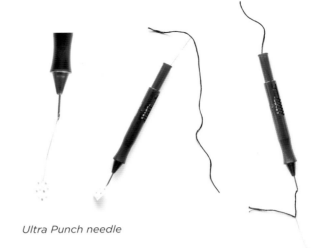

Ultra Punch needle

Tip: If you are using the stitch side as your front (the side you are seeing), pull the yarn tail through to the back on the first punch. This gives a cleaner finish!

Insert the needle all the way down into the backing cloth. If you don't, the loops will be inconsistent and might even come out.

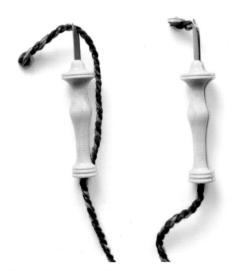

Oxford punch needle

Push all the way down.

On the Ultra Punch needle, insert the threader through the needle up to the top. Thread the floss or yarn and pull through. The open front of the needle should face the direction you are punching. Once threaded, pull the yarn so that it doesn't have any slack and it sits nicely in the needle.

Tip: If you're working with slippery yarns or floss, use your free hand to hold the stitches on the back as you punch. Don't pull them though or the loops will also be inconsistent. I also always outline a section first and then fill it in; the outline guides me and gives me a nice tight shape. If I'm working on the background, I also do the same—outline and then fill in the rest.

Slowly take out the needle, but don't lift too much! Graze the surface of the backing cloth as you place your needle for the next punch. If you lift the needle too high, you will pull the yarn and undo the stitch. This process might take a little bit of practice, but before you know it your muscle memory will kick in and you'll be punching faster.

Don't pull the needle this high, the stitch will come out!

Be sure to make your stitches consistent in size. Refer to Stitch Length & Troubleshooting for more details (page 20).

If you need to stop or change colors, pull the needle out slowly and cut the yarn as close as you can to the backing cloth. If I am using the stitch side as the front, I always poke the end through to the other side.

What You Need to Remember
- Don't pull the needle too high.
- Don't have any tension on your yarn or floss.
- Make your stitches consistent.

These steps will ensure that your piece is made of tightly packed loops and stitches that will hold it together! If you have any pulls later on, check out my felting needle trick on page 20 to fix small imperfections.

Blooming Apron (page 85)

STITCH LENGTH & TROUBLESHOOTING

The Oxford rug hooking punch needle comes with a handy stitch gauge that will guide you with a 1-inch (2.5-cm) hole. You can also make your own by cutting out a 1-inch (2.5-cm) window on a bookmark or piece of cardboard.

If you're using a thick yarn, you should be punching four stitches per running inch (2.5 cm). For a thinner yarn, you should be punching six stiches per running inch (2.5 cm). You'll get a feel for the yarn you're using as you work, and you'll know if you need to adjust the length of your stitches.

I use a tighter stitch length when I'm outlining shapes or punching flower stems as it gives me a fuller look. As you're punching, you want to stagger the rows of stitches; this will fill in any gaps in between. I turn my work often to check if my rows are consistent. If the backing cloth is showing through on the loop side, it means that I'm not measuring the stitch length correctly and my spacing is too big for the thickness of the yarn.

Gauging the length of the stitches on the embroidery punch needle is a bit trickier as the stitches are tiny. It also varies depending on the thickness of the floss or yarn you're using. I find myself using 1.5 to 2 mm stitches. Whatever size you choose, keep it consistent and always check for loop height.

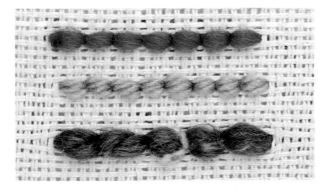

Length of stitches according to the yarn thickness.

FIXING MISTAKES & ACCIDENTS

One of the things I love most about punch needle is the fact that it's really forgiving if you make a mistake. When I first started punching and I was unhappy with my designs, I would pull out the yarn and start all over. The monk's cloth allowed me to do this easily; rubbing it with your nail or the back of the punch needle allows you to "heal" the cloth.

When you are done punching, trim any loose ends and loops that are oversized. If you are using the loop side as your front, you'll notice sometimes that the loops are out of place. This is especially noticeable if you're punching stems or lines. Simply push them into place by using a skewer or the end of your scissors—just be careful not to pull though!

From time to time some loops get caught and they pull out, or a pet gets ahold of a piece and does some damage. The good news is that most small pulls can be repaired. I use a felting needle to push in any loose loops or stitches. Simply poke the yarn back in and the snag will be virtually invisible. Always have a felting needle handy just in case.

FINISHING YOUR PIECE

Always trim any long or loose pieces after you've finished punching. You want your work to be as clean as possible.

You'll notice your piece will curve and roll when you take it off the frame. Setting it with a hot iron and a wet cloth or towel for about 10 seconds will flatten it out and make the loops even. Be very careful when using acrylic and synthetic yarns as the heat will melt them! I don't find that embroidery pieces need to be set as the floss is very thin and it doesn't really affect the integrity of the piece.

Will it become undone? Generally speaking, no. A properly made piece should be strong enough to resist normal use without having to seal the back. Having said that, if you have pets—especially cats—I recommend keeping your pieces away from them. The only time I suggest sealing the back is when you use the small embroidery punch needle. The embroidery floss is too thin and slippery; it can come out easily. These pieces are also more likely to be washed so sealing them is a good idea. You'll see a note in the projects where I recommend sealing, and you can see the technique on page 123.

Always trim any loose ends.

Use a felting needle to push back any loose loops.

Use a skewer or a sharp tip to untangle misplaced loops.

WALL ART

Punch needle gives you the freedom to create pieces with great detail. Some call it painting with yarn. I find this to be absolutely true and a great way to approach a wall art piece. It's also the perfect way to add some excitement to any bare walls or add an element of texture to existing gallery walls.

If you ever find yourself unsure of what to do with a punch piece, chances are you can turn it into a wall hanging. If you used a canvas stretcher and stapled your backing cloth to the frame, you've got an instant art piece. The Monarca Wall Art piece (page 45) will show you how to finish it on the frame. Wall art is also great to use any kind of yarn you have laying around; because it won't be handled you don't need to worry about it outlasting wear and tear. Grab your favorites and explore new color schemes.

Some of these projects use hoops as the stretcher frame, which works wonders for a ready-to-hang piece. Vintage hoops would be lovely here as would thin pieces of driftwood for hanging tapestries. Have fun with it!

FLOR HANGING HOOP

Finished size: 14" (35.5 cm) in diameter

Working with an embroidery hoop as your stretcher frame makes for a really easy and accessible project to start with. Hoops are readily available, and you can size up or down to suit the space you want your piece to hang in. Mexican kitchens frequently display imagery of fruit and flowers. Paintings, tableware and utensils often combine this playful theme. Strawberries are a favorite in my house—they are always ready to enjoy!

BEFORE YOU START

For this project, I opted to paint the monk's cloth that shows on the edge to avoid having a visible gap between the yarn and hoop. If you choose to do the same, use a thin acrylic paint and a stiff brush. For pieces where my front is the side, I prefer using the size 14 mini needle to save yarn. In this project, the flower is punched through the back to add texture with the loops on the front, if you have a fine yarn you can use a size 10 fine needle. I used a size 10 regular as my yarn was a little thicker.

MATERIALS

- 14" × 14" (35.5 × 35.5 cm) monk's cloth, 13 thread count, plus enough to wrap around your frame (See the Stretcher Frames section, page 16.)
- Template
- Carbon paper
- Matching dark blue acrylic paint (optional)
- Approximately 1 oz (28 g) of each color of medium-weight wool yarn in dark blue, yellow, 2 shades of red, 2 shades of pink and 4 shades of green

TOOLS

- 14" (35.5-cm) embroidery hoop
- Hot glue gun
- Soft pencil
- Stiff paintbrush (hog hair; optional)
- Size 14 mini and size 10 fine or regular Oxford punch needle
- Scissors

YARN COLORS

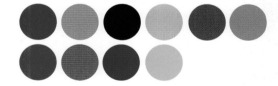

1

2

PUNCHING THE DESIGN

1. Lay your embroidery hoop on your monk's cloth. Start folding the fabric in around the hoop. Apply hot glue in a small section and fold down until it sets. Keep stretching the fabric in opposite directions so the hoop doesn't warp. Do not use too much glue in case you need to readjust.

   Tip: Glue small sections at a time. This will give you a more even stretch all around and you will avoid getting folds on the edges of the hoop. If you do have folds, simply pull off the fabric and readjust. If you find it's not coming off, use a hair dryer to warm up the glue. You can also use the outer frame hoop to cover this if you wish.

2. Transfer the pattern by placing the carbon paper underneath the pattern template and tracing over it with a soft pencil. Be sure to apply constant pressure.

   After I've traced the pattern, I like to paint the monk's cloth that sits directly on top of the hoop (the part you can't punch on) so that I don't see a gap between the yarn and the outer hoop. This step is completely optional; you might like to see the gap! If you are painting it, take a stiff brush and lightly paint over the outer edge with a paint that matches or is close to the color of the background. On my hoop it was less than ¼ inch (6.4 mm). Don't paint more than you need and don't do a thick coat. Less is more! Let it dry completely for a couple of hours.

3

4

3. With the dark pink yarn, punch the outline of the flower and the line that goes through each petal.

   With the light pink, punch the middle highlights of each petal.

4. Flip your hoop so that you are now punching through the back and punch the rest of each petal with the dark pink. Still punching through the back, punch the center of the flower with yellow yarn.

5

5. Flip your hoop again and punch the flower stem with lime green, then the big leaf and one half of the small leaf with the light shade of green. Punch the other half of the small leaf with the dark green. With another shade of green, punch the stems of the strawberries.

   Punch the strawberries with a light red in the center and dark red on the outside.

   To finish your hoop, punch the background with the dark blue yarn. You're done!

CAMPO HANGING HOOP

Finished size: 18" (45.7 cm) in diameter

In Mexico, the flower has always been symbolic and present in our culture. From pottery to textiles to clothing, the flower expresses many years of history and diversity. This piece reminds me of a flower field (campo), and it's one of my favorites. The Ultra Punch needle is excellent for the fine details found in florals. It allows you to get sharp lines and corners as well as a gradation of color in your work. For this pattern, you will be working on both the front and back for a mix of textures. Don't be afraid to mix and match colors that you wouldn't normally use together.

BEFORE YOU START

We will be working with different tones of embroidery floss to create the gradients in the flowers. I recommend using three tones of each color to get a nice even transition. The use of a water-soluble transfer pen is optional, but it might come in handy as you will be tracing the design on both sides of the fabric.

MATERIALS

- Template
- 18" × 18" (45.7 × 45.7 cm) natural linen fabric, plus enough to wrap around your hoop
- Approximately 2 skeins of embroidery floss of each color in 3 shades of red, 4 shades of pink, 2 shades of light pink, 2 shades of yellow, 2 shades of blue and green
- 1 skein each of lightweight dark and light green yarn
- No-sew permanent fabric adhesive

TOOLS

- Heat transfer pen
- Iron
- 18" (45.7-cm) embroidery hoop
- Hot glue gun
- Soft pencil (optional)
- Ultra Punch punch needle tool with medium and large needles
- Water-soluble transfer pen (optional)
- Scissors
- Stiff paintbrush (hog hair)

FLOSS COLORS

YARN COLORS

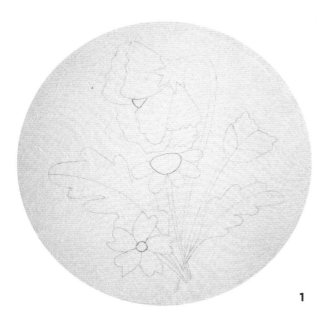

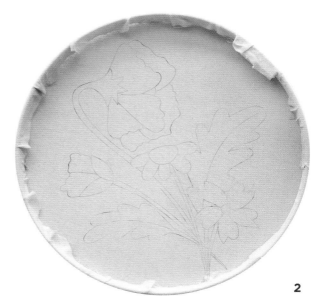

1

2

PUNCHING THE DESIGN

1. Transfer the pattern by drawing over the template with a heat transfer pen. Place the pattern on top of your fabric and iron the pattern into place. Remember that the lines will be permanent so pay close attention to placement.

   With the design facing down and centered, lay the embroidery frame on top. Fold the fabric in and glue it in place. Continue on the opposite side, stretching the fabric. Do not use too much glue in case you need to readjust. Keep stretching the fabric consistently and switching directions so the hoop doesn't warp.

   Tip: Glue small sections at a time. This will give you a more even stretch all around and you will avoid getting folds on the edges of the hoop. If you do have folds, simply pull off the fabric and readjust. If you find it's not coming off, use a hair dryer to warm up the glue. You can also use the outer frame hoop to cover this if you wish.

2. Once you've traced your pattern on the front, it's time to trace it on the back. Take your hoop and hold it against the light. You might have to play with the angle; holding it straight up or against a window didn't work for me as well as holding it at a slight slant. If you find the transfer isn't dark enough, retrace it with a soft lead pencil or use the transfer pen and then flip to trace.

3. Using the medium needle set to number 5 in the length adjustment, start by punching the center of the flowers on the back of the hoop. Use four strands of your embroidery floss of mixed yellow tones. I used two strands of a darker yellow and two of a lighter yellow.

   Tip: Embroidery floss tends to "fluff" up a bit more than yarn, therefore you may want to make your stitches slightly bigger (about 4 mm long).

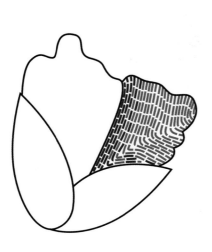

3

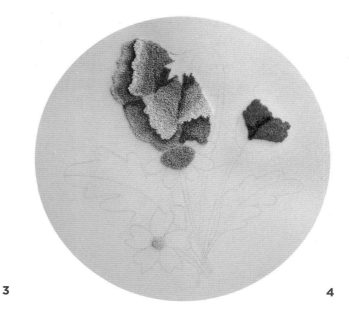

4

For the red bloom, I created a shadow between both petals by taking three strands of dark red floss and punching the left petal first. Remember you're looking at the back, so the left petal is really the right petal. Punch three lines of dark red. Take two strands of dark red and one of lighter red and continue punching to start creating the gradient. Finish by using three strands of light red for the rest of the petal.

There is no specific count to this; it's by feel. If you'd like a bit more of a shadow, continue with the dark red. If not, start lightening it up. The important thing here is to mix the strands of colors so there are no harsh lines when you transition from one shade to another. I find that punching in curved lines rather than straight lines gives a more natural look.

Tip: You can also adjust the colors with the quantity of strands you use. For example, to go from dark to light use three strands of dark

to start, then two strands of dark and one of light, then two strands of light and one of dark, then finally three strands of light.

For the second petal, I used a lighter red near the tip as a highlight.

4. Continue to punch the largest flower using the same technique. Tackle one front petal at a time. I used four different shades of pink for the gradient as they are larger petals. The petals in the front should be lighter in color than the petals on the back.

Change the length of the needle to number 3. Finish the flower by punching the back petals using mostly darker shades.

5

6

5. Change the needle to the larger size and change the length to number 7. If you use anything shorter, you risk the yarn coming out as you punch. Thread the needle with the lightweight dark green yarn and outline the larger flower's stem before filling it in. Continue with the rest of the stems.

Continue punching both leaves. Use the dark green for one half of the leaves and punch the second half with the light green.

Tip: If you don't have a lightweight yarn, use six strands of embroidery floss; it's about the same thickness.

6. To punch the daisy petals, change the medium needle length to number 5. I used two shades of a really light blush pink and alternated the colors. Instead of making short stitches, you are going to punch once on the edge of the petal and then another time on the opposite edge. Do this back and forth until you cover the whole petal, varying the length of the

stiches to accommodate for the curved tip. As you are punching, it might be helpful to hold the floss loop underneath the hoop as you pull the needle to the other side. Floss can be slippery, and it doesn't hurt to hold it in case you pull harder than you need to.

Tip: If you find the threads to be loose, flip the hoop so you are looking at the back and pull the loops on both sides at the same time. This will tighten the stitch. Don't pull only one side as you will risk the other side coming undone.

Continue with the same technique for the blue flower. For the widest parts of the petals, instead of punching from one edge to the other, punch halfway in the middle and then continue to the other side. This will prevent the stitch from being too loose. Continue punching, but stagger your middle stitch so that it doesn't align with your previous one. This will give you more of a seamless look.

7. Once you're finished it's time to seal the stitches. Note that this step is only needed for the last two flowers you punched as the stitches are too loose to leave as is. Follow the directions on page 123 to seal them, and you're done!

BOTANICAL WALL HANGING

Finished size: 16" × 30" (40.6 × 76.2 cm)

One of my favorite characteristics of long Mexican textile pieces is that the motifs are often mirrored or symmetrical. I find it creates a harmonious design that is quite pleasing to the eye. Mexican designs are recognizable as they feature multicolored flowers in a variety of styles, as well as greenery that fills the space. Many flowers take on an abstract form that is not a specific representation of a particular species. I love that artisans take liberties creating something that speaks to them and that complements their style. For this wall hanging, I added some fun tassels to extend its height and add another texture element to the piece.

BEFORE YOU START

This is a project that works with any size of punch needle and any type of yarn. Because this is a piece that won't be handled, we don't have to worry about using only wool yarn. Feel free to use any thickness or material you want. Measure a space you'd like to fill and add the tassels for a fun look!

MATERIALS

- 16" × 30" (40.6 × 76.2 cm) monk's cloth, 13 thread count, plus enough to wrap around your frame (See the Stretcher Frames section, page 16.)
- Template
- Carbon paper
- Approximately 1 oz (28 g) of each color of medium-weight wool yarn in 2 shades of pink, yellow, brown, 3 shades of blue, 3 shades of green, 3 shades of magenta and 10 oz (283 g) of speckled cream yarn
- White or cream-colored sewing thread
- 4" x 3½" (10 x 9–cm) piece of cardboard

TOOLS

- Sewing machine (optional)
- Fabric stretcher frame
- Soft pencil
- Size 14 mini Oxford punch needle
- Scissors
- Sewing needle
- Pins
- Iron
- Wet cloth
- One 17" (48.3-cm) dowel
- 25" (63.5 cm) cotton twine

YARN COLORS

PUNCHING THE DESIGN

1. To prevent the monk's cloth from unraveling, zigzag the edges using a sewing machine and thread. If you don't have a sewing machine, you can skip this step.

   Stretch the monk's cloth tightly over your stretcher frame. Make sure it's taut and wrinkle-free.

Transfer the pattern by placing the carbon paper underneath the pattern template and tracing over it with a soft pencil. Be sure to apply constant pressure.

Start by punching the flower stems in dark green. Punch three rows for the yellow bud stems and four rows for the rest of the stems. Continue with the leaves in two different tones of green.

3

4

2. Continue punching the pink flowers by starting with the light pink and following with the dark pink.

    Next, punch the yellow flowers and brown centers.

3. With your three different shades of magenta, punch the middle flowers starting with the light color and moving outwards to the darker colors.

Lastly, punch the blue flower using your three shades of blue.

4. Once all your floral elements are done, it's time to punch the background. Use the speckled cream-colored yarn to finish your piece.

5

6

7

8

5. Trim any loose or long ends on the back and take your piece off the frame. Fix any large holes made by the frame on the monk's cloth around the edges using a sewing needle or your punch tool.

   Trim the monk's cloth around the edges to 1½ inches (3.8 cm) all around.

   Iron your piece using the high temperature setting. To do this, take a wet (not dripping) cloth and place it on top of the loop side. Iron it, applying slight pressure. This will flatten your piece and take care of any uneven loops.

To hem the edges of your wall hanging follow the steps on page 120.

6. Make 15 tassels, all different colors that coordinate with your piece. To make a tassel, use a piece of cardboard to wrap the yarn around tightly. Wrap as many times as you'd like to achieve the fullness you want the tassel to have. Thread a 15-inch (38-cm)-long piece of yarn through the top loops and tie firmly. Leave a long end so that you can braid it. Slide the yarn off the cardboard and cut the loose loops. Use another piece of yarn to tie the "head". Trim the ends and tuck them into the tassel.

9

10

7. Once you have the combination of colors you'd like to use, arrange the tassels in groups of three. Take the second tassel and thread the end through your upholstery needle. Pass the needle through the center of the tassel that sits on top and pull the yarn through. Do the same for the third tassel passing through the second and then the first. All three strands should be together now.

8. Space out the tassels so that they hang close together. Once positioned braid all three strands together.

9. Lay your piece flat and space out each of the 5 tassels so that they spread out evenly across the piece. Feel free to play with height; you can also hang them all at the same height. Hand stitch them to the back once you're happy with it.

10. Snip two or three stitches on the top two corners of the monk's cloth. Insert your dowel through the top and bottom hem and center it so that there is a little bit hanging off each end.

Lastly, tie your cotton twine around each end of the dowel and hang. You're finished!

ALCATRAZ WALL HANGING

Finished size: 13" × 27" (33 × 68.5 cm)

Calla lilies, aside from being my favorite, are a popular flower in Mexican culture. Famous artists such as Diego Rivera have made them a popular icon by including them in their paintings. Throughout the years, the calla lily has made an appearance in paintings, textiles, pottery and many other traditional Mexican crafts. Their simple elegance makes them an ideal shape, and this wall hanging would fit in well in any modern home.

BEFORE YOU START

This piece plays with texture and dimension. I used a short and long punch needle to give it some more interest. The size 14 mini can be used to give sections some depth. For example, the "inside" of the calla lily can be punched with the smaller needle, while the longer punch needle can be used for the petals that sit on top so that they are raised. Feel free to experiment—there is no right or wrong! You can also just use one size if you prefer. If you have more than five different shades of blue, I would encourage you to use them. This is a great pattern to practice color combination and balance. For the finishing touch, adding a polyester trim is completely optional though it can add a bit more excitement and height if you need it. I chose to use premade trim, but you can make it yourself just as easily using leftover yarn from your piece.

MATERIALS

- 13" x 27" (33 x 68.5 cm) monk's cloth, 13 thread count, plus enough to wrap around your frame (See the Stretcher Frames section, page 16.)
- Template
- Carbon paper
- Approximately 1½ oz (44 g) of each color of medium-weight wool yarn in 5 shades of blue and 5 oz (142 g) of white
- White or cream-colored thread
- 16" (40.6 cm) of trim in blue and 16" (40.6 cm) of trim in white (optional)

TOOLS

- Sewing machine (optional)
- Fabric stretcher frame
- Soft pencil
- Size 14 mini and size 10 fine Oxford punch needle
- Scissors
- Sewing needle
- Iron
- Wet cloth
- One 17" (48.3-cm) dowel
- 25" (63.5 cm) cotton twine, for hanging

YARN COLORS

1a

1b

■ *Size 10 fine*
■ *Size 14 mini*

PUNCHING THE DESIGN

1. To prevent the monk's cloth from unraveling, zigzag the edges using a sewing machine and thread. If you don't have a sewing machine, you can skip this step.

   Stretch the monk's cloth tightly over your stretcher frame. Make sure it's taut and wrinkle-free.

   Transfer the pattern by placing the carbon paper underneath the pattern template and tracing over it with a soft pencil. Be sure to apply constant pressure.

   Start punching the design. While there is no particular order to follow, I recommend punching the same size/color together to save the time it takes to re-thread the needle. Remember that changing the needle size is not necessary, but if you choose to do so, you can follow my pattern recommendations.

   Once you've punched the floral design, carefully take your piece off the frame and flip it so that you are now looking at the loop side. Carefully stretch it over your stretcher frame so that it's taut.

   Punch the background using white yarn. This will give your design a raised look even if you chose not to use different needles.

2

3

2. Trim any loose or long ends on the back and take your piece off the frame. Fix any large holes made by the frame on the monk's cloth around the edges using a sewing needle or your punch tool.

Trim the monk's cloth around the edges to 1½ inches (3.8 cm) all around.

Iron your piece using the high temperature setting. To do this, take a wet (not dripping) cloth and place it on top of the loop side. Iron it, applying slight pressure. This will flatten your piece and take care of any uneven loops.

To finish the edges of your wall hanging follow the steps on page 120. If you are adding trim, I suggest not binding the bottom edge.

3. Snip two or three stitches on the top two corners. Insert your dowel through the hem and center it so that there is a little bit hanging off each end. Lastly, tie your cotton twine around each end of the dowel and hang. You're finished!

Optional: If you are adding the trim, hand-sew or machine-sew it to the bottom of your piece.

MONARCA WALL ART

Finished size: 20" × 16" (50.8 × 40.6 cm)

Millions of Monarch butterflies arrive in Mexico every November after their long trip from Canada. Though I didn't live where the butterflies congregate at the end of their trip, I remember the skies being filled with them in the fall as they traveled to their final destination. Here in Canada when I see them in the late summer, I'm reminded of where they are heading. Butterflies have been important symbols in Aztec and Mayan art, representing love, freedom, femininity and sensuality. Design this piece however you want to; use my piece as a guide, but feel free to add or subtract from it.

BEFORE YOU START

I wanted to include a piece that gets you thinking about design and space. Feel free to make this piece as simple or as complicated as you like. I chose to add some texture and shapes to the background, but you can do it all one color if you'd prefer. The trick to having the background not take over the butterflies is to keep it all within the green family. Pick tones that are close to each other so that they don't become too distracting. You can use any type of yarn you want; this is a piece that will be hung and will not be handled. I bought the stretcher bars on their own, but you can also use a pre-stretched canvas, just remove the canvas cloth and only use the frame. I used my 18" × 18" (45.7 × 45.7-cm) stretcher frame for this piece then shifted it to add on to the edges.

MATERIALS

- 20" × 16" (50.8 × 40.6 cm) monk's cloth, 13 thread count, plus enough to wrap around your frame (See the Stretcher Frames section, page 16.)
- Template
- Carbon paper
- Approximately 2 oz (57 g) of each color of medium-weight yarn in orange, black, ½ oz (14 g) of white and 3½ oz (99 g) of green if you're doing a flat background, otherwise 1 oz (28 g) of each of the colors you plan to use
- 20" × 16" (50.8 × 40.6-cm) canvas frame
- Dark green acrylic paint (optional)

TOOLS

- Sewing machine (optional)
- Fabric stretcher frame
- Soft pencil
- Size 14 mini, 10 regular and 10 fine Oxford punch needles
- Scissors
- Sewing needle
- Staple gun
- Stiff paintbrush (hog hair; optional)

YARN COLORS

PUNCHING THE DESIGN

1. To prevent the monk's cloth from unraveling, zigzag the edges using a sewing machine and thread. If you don't have a sewing machine, you can skip this step.

    Stretch the monk's cloth tightly over your stretcher frame. Make sure it's taut and wrinkle-free.

    Punch the outline of the stretcher frame you want to cover so that you know your working space.

    Transfer the butterfly pattern by placing the carbon paper underneath the pattern template and tracing over it with a soft pencil. Be sure to apply constant pressure. Feel free to cut out the butterfly and outline the outside. You're designing your own pattern—have fun with it!

    Using the size 14 mini needle, start by punching the edges, body and outlines in black. I punched some of the lines with a single line and others with two. Feel free to experiment, but always make sure that what you do on one side you do on the other.

2. Punch the remaining parts in orange. Once that is done, thread the white yarn and punch the white spots and antenna.

    Note: This is the only time I'll advise you to overlap stitches because it is such a small area. I also like the spotted look it gives. You don't need to overdo it—a couple of stitches will go a long way.

    Continue these steps for the rest of the butterflies.

3

4

3. Once you're done punching all the butterflies, finish by punching the background, switching colors and alternating needle sizes. This is where you get to go wild. Experiment with different shapes and sizes and change the size of the punch needle. Do whatever feels natural to you! If you don't feel adventurous just yet, punch the background in one shade of green.

4. Trim any loose or long ends on the back and take your piece off the frame. Fix any large holes made by the frame on the monk's cloth around the edges using a needle or your punch tool.

   Lay your finished piece on top of the canvas frame and stretch your punched piece in place. Secure with staples.

5

5. Because I don't like how the monk's cloth shows on the sides, I painted it using the acrylic paint and stiff brush. This step is totally optional and up to you. Let it dry completely overnight and your wall piece is ready to hang!

PILLOWS & RUGS

The first item I made when I got a punch needle was a pillow. I wanted something different to spice up my living room, so I picked up yarn in colors that matched my other pillows and away I went. Punch needle is easily adaptable to any décor by coordinating colors to the existing palettes in your home.

One of the things I love most about Mexican décor is how bright and beautiful the color choices are. Do not be afraid to mix and match, especially when these items can be easily rotated according to the seasons. Growing up, I remember admiring my childhood friend's home; her mom always showcased large traditional artisanal wares as focal points. Whether it was a ceramic piece or a large embroidered pillow, the items surrounding it always picked up on the colors.

In this section, you'll find projects that will add the finishing touch to any setup you have going on in your home. Make these projects the focal point or have them coordinate with your current pieces. A pillow is a great way to work your way up to a large wall hanging or a stunning rug. Because most of these items will experience day-to-day wear, search for wool or wool-blend yarns as they will hold up to the wear and tear specifically when it comes to rugs. Feel free to change up the colors or use part of some of the patterns to make your own design!

TALAVERA PILLOW

Finished size: 18″ × 18″ (45.7 × 45.7 cm)

Talavera is a popular pottery style in the cities of Puebla, Atlixco, Cholula and Tecali. It's named after the Spanish Queen or the "Queen's Talavera" and typically has a white base. Artisans are only permitted to use six colors—indigo, yellow, green, orange, black and a dusty pink—though the majority of this pottery can be found using only indigo. I remember my mom always searching for the "right" set to use during family gatherings and special occasions. Though truth be told once she found it, she was scared to use it. Searching for the right design and balance of colors can be quite the endeavor! Many Mexican families take pride in displaying their Talavera. It's handmade, and the more intricate the design, the pricier it is. Just like the majority of the Talavera designs out there, this pattern has a symmetrical floral motif that can be easily adapted to a circular shape.

BEFORE YOU START

Because we will be using the flat side that you see as you're punching, you want to use a needle that has a short tip to minimize the amount of yarn you'll need. The 14 mini needle is perfect for this. Because of its fine tip, you'll need a thin or medium-weight yarn. I used a speckled yarn for this to add some interest. If you are unable to find one you can use a cream or white color for the background. Wool yarn or a wool blend is recommended for durability. Feel free to adapt this project to a circular design. If you're comfortable drawing, you can use the flower and leaves as your center and tweak the elements around them to form a circle.

MATERIALS

- 18″ × 18″ (45.7 × 45.7 cm) monk's cloth, 13 thread count, plus enough to wrap around your frame (See the Stretcher Frames section, page 16.)
- Template
- Carbon paper
- Approximately 5 oz (142 g) of each color of medium-weight wool in dark blue and speckled cream yarn
- 2 (19″ × 14″ [48.3 × 35.5-cm]) pieces of matching fabric for the back of the pillow
- Matching thread
- 18″ × 18″ (45.7 × 45.7-cm) pillow form

TOOLS

- Sewing machine (optional)
- Fabric stretcher frame
- Soft pencil
- Water-soluble pen
- Size 14 mini Oxford punch needle
- Scissors
- Pins or sewing clips

YARN COLORS

PUNCHING THE DESIGN

1. To prevent the monk's cloth from unraveling, zigzag the edges using a sewing machine and thread. This is optional but well worth it!

   Stretch the monk's cloth tightly over your stretcher frame. Make sure it's taut and wrinkle-free.

   Transfer the pattern by placing the carbon paper underneath the pattern template and tracing over it with a soft pencil. Be sure to apply constant pressure.

   Tip: Make sure the design is centered; this is a symmetrical design and you want to make sure all your lines are straight. Touch up any lines with a pencil or water-soluble pen.

   Start by punching the flower in the middle. It's always a good starting point and serves as a reference point as you punch the rest of the design.

2. Continue punching the rest of the design. Remember that you are seeing the front of your pillow; make your stitches even, staggered and consistent in size. Don't be afraid to make smaller stitches as you get close to a corner; an inconsistent stitch is preferable to an overlapping stitch. Stop, cut the thread and start again as needed. You'll find that you might need to do this often for this project.

3. Punch the background with the speckled yarn.

   Once finished, flip over the frame and trim any loose or long ends.

   Take your piece off the frame.

   Using the 19 × 14–inch (48.3 × 35.5–cm) fabric pieces, follow the instructions on page 122 to complete the rest of your pillow.

FIESTA RECTANGLE PILLOW

Finished size: 26" × 16" (66 × 40.6 cm)

Mexican party décor is always extra colorful. Flags and striking garlands are almost always a staple at any party. Vibrant and contrasting color schemes that wouldn't normally match sing when paired together. Color has a way of evoking happiness: the brighter the better. This pillow, whether on the bed or the sofa, is sure to offer some brightness to your space.

BEFORE YOU START

This project mixes and matches needle sizes. Feel free to mix and match yarn weights for an even more interesting result. Working with variegated yarn is a fun way of incorporating more color without having to switch back and forth between yarn. When looking for a variegated yarn for this project look for one that has a subtle gradient of colors; working with a yarn that contrasts too much will give you a different look. The key is to keep it within the same color family.

MATERIALS

- 26" × 16" (66 × 40.6 cm) monk's cloth, 13 thread count, plus enough to wrap around your frame (See the Stretcher Frames section, page 16.)
- Template
- Carbon paper
- Approximately 1½ oz (43 g) of each color of medium-weight wool yarn in cream, light blue, blue, heavyweight wool yarn in yellow and red, and 5 oz (142 g) of variegated red yarn
- 2 (17" × 18" [48.3 × 45.7–cm]) pieces of matching fabric for the back of the pillow
- Matching thread
- 26" × 16" (66 × 40.6–cm) pillow form

TOOLS

- Sewing machine (optional)
- Fabric stretcher frame
- Soft pencil
- Size 14 mini, size 10 fine and regular Oxford punch needle
- Scissors
- Pins or sewing clips

YARN COLORS

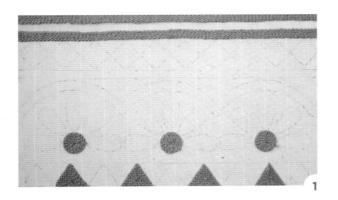

PUNCHING THE DESIGN

1. To prevent the monk's cloth from unraveling, zigzag the edges using a sewing machine and thread. This is optional but well worth it!

   Stretch the monk's cloth tightly over your stretcher frame. Make sure it's taut and wrinkle-free.

   Transfer the pattern by placing the carbon paper underneath the pattern template and tracing over it with a soft pencil. Be sure to apply constant pressure.

   Begin punching the yellow sections with the size 10 needle. I used a thick yarn and the regular size 10 needle.

2. With a size 10 fine needle, punch the red variegated sections.

3. Switch to the 14 mini needle to punch the blue, light blue and cream sections.

4. Finish punching your piece by switching to the size 10. I used a regular size. Punch the red diamonds on the top.

   Using the 26 × 16-inch (66 × 40.6-cm) fabric pieces, follow the instructions on page 122 to complete the rest of your pillow.

TENEK PILLOW

Finished size: 18" × 18" (45.7 × 45.7 cm)

Growing up in Mexico, I had the opportunity to become exposed to all kinds of embroidery. Cross-stitch is usually the preferred way to learn how to embroider because it's relatively easy. The complexity can be brought in as the pattern gets more elaborate. The traditional Tenek embroidery design originates from the state of San Luis Potosí in Huehuetlán. Traditionally made using cross-stitch embroidery, the Tenek imagery often depicts flowers, a star that symbolizes the tree of life and animals native to the region in bright lively colors. The traditional colors are pink or red for blood, orange for the sun and green for the trees. Many artisan women choose their own combinations and often add contrasting colors to make the embroidery their own. This pillow will bring a colorful touch to your décor while embracing both the geometric and floral characteristics of Tenek embroidery.

BEFORE YOU START

You can use any size needle you'd like, but it must be a "fine" tip. Make sure the frame you're using has the inside dimensions of 18" × 18" (45.7 × 45.7 cm) that you can punch through. The amount of yarn used depends on your punching style and the needle size you're using. I used less than one whole skein for the background. The amount for the rest of the colors is minimal in comparison. Wool yarn or a wool blend is recommended for durability.

MATERIALS

- 18" × 18" (45.7 × 45.7 cm) monk's cloth, 13 thread count, plus enough to wrap around your frame (See the Stretcher Frames section, page 16.)
- Template
- Carbon paper
- Approximately 4 oz (113 g) of each color of medium-weight wool yarn in dark pink, light pink, dark orange, light orange, dark green, light green, dark lime, light lime and cream
- 2 (19" × 14" [48.3 × 35.5–cm]) pieces of matching fabric for the back of the pillow
- Matching thread
- 18" × 18" (45.7 × 45.7–cm) pillow form

TOOLS

- Sewing machine (optional)
- Fabric stretcher frame
- Soft pencil
- Pencil or water-soluble pen
- Size 10 fine Oxford punch needle
- Scissors
- Pins or sewing clips

YARN COLORS

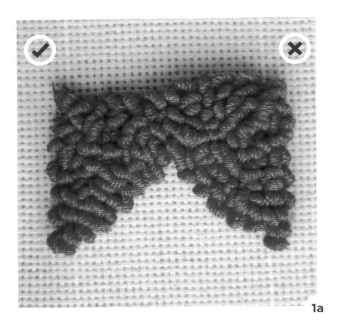

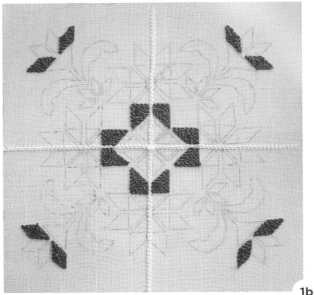

1a

1b

Don't overpunch; space out your stitches so that you retain your shapes.

PUNCHING THE DESIGN

1. To prevent the monk's cloth from unraveling, zigzag the edges using a sewing machine and thread. This is optional but well worth it!

    Stretch the monk's cloth tightly over your stretcher frame. Make sure it's taut and wrinkle-free.

    Transfer the pattern by placing the carbon paper underneath the pattern template and tracing over it with a soft pencil. Be sure to apply constant pressure.

    Tip: Make sure the design is centered; because this is a symmetrical design you want to make sure all your lines are straight. Touch up any lines with a pencil or water-soluble pen.

Start by punching the middle intersecting lines using the cream-colored (background) yarn. They should be two rows thick. This will give you a grid reference that you can follow as you punch the rest of the shapes.

Punch the dark pink shapes. This will give you a feel for how the shapes will fill in with the yarn.

Note: Because the shapes are small in scale, be sure not to overpunch. Space the punches evenly so that you don't end up with a dense shape that can easily overcrowd the other colors.

2

3

2. Continue punching the background lines.

   Tip: Be sure to stagger your stitches, otherwise you will have empty spots in your outline. A good tip is to punch more stitches per inch (2.5 cm), so you end up with a fuller line.

3. Finish by punching the different colored shapes and the rest of the background.

   Tip: It's much faster to do all the same-colored shapes at once to minimize trimming and threading of the needle.

   Once finished, trim any long threads and fix any loops that might be out of place.

   Take your piece off the frame.

   Using the 19 × 14-inch (48.3 × 35.5-cm) fabric pieces, follow the instructions on page 122 to complete the rest of your pillow.

TAMAULIPECA RUG

Finished size: 30" × 20" (76.2 × 50.8 cm)

I started to study Mexican folk dancing when I was about ten years old. I've always been fascinated by the beautiful costumes and elaborate hair pieces. This year, I learned some dances from the state of Tamaulipas. The traditional regional attire depicts simple stylized flowers and vines that adorn shirts, dresses, suede jackets and pants. The flowers used represent the anacahuita or Mexican olive plant that is found and grown in the states of Tamaulipas. Known as its official flower, the anacahuita bushes flower year-round, making it a very attractive plant. This design is inspired by a dress I've worn, a bright turquoise blue dress with multiple flower accents that will light up any space.

BEFORE YOU START

I made my own stretcher frame with carpet strips. It's probably the most economical way to make such a large frame. Be careful though, it can get very sharp! Be sure to cover the tacks with felt or thick fabric. Wool yarn or a wool blend is recommended for durability in this project as it will get a lot of traffic. Section off your punching so that you see progress quicker— it's easy to get discouraged if no sections are being "filled in."

MATERIALS

- 30" × 20" (76.2 × 50.8 cm) monk's cloth, 13 thread count, plus enough to wrap around your frame (See the Stretcher Frames section, page 16.)
- Template
- Carbon paper
- Approximately 11 oz (312 g) of medium-weight wool yarn in turquoise and 3½ oz (99 g) of yellow
- Yellow or cream-colored thread

TOOLS

- Sewing machine (optional)
- Fabric stretcher frame
- Soft pencil
- Size 10 regular Oxford punch needle
- Scissors
- Sewing needle
- Pins
- Iron
- Wet cloth

YARN COLORS

PUNCHING THE DESIGN

1. To prevent the monk's cloth from unraveling, zigzag the edges using a sewing machine and thread. If you don't have a sewing machine, you can skip this step.

    Stretch the monk's cloth tightly over your stretcher frame. Make sure it's taut and wrinkle-free.

    Transfer the pattern by placing the carbon paper underneath the pattern template and tracing over it with a soft pencil. Be sure to apply constant pressure.

    Start by punching the flower motif in yellow.

2. Continue punching the rest of the background in turquoise. Since punching a large piece like this can get overwhelming, I like to section off the background so I can fill little sections at a time. I find it more rewarding and it makes the project go by quicker.

    Once finished, trim any loose or long ends on the back and take your piece off the frame. Fix any large holes made by the frame on the monk's cloth around the edges using a needle or your punch tool.

    Trim the monk's cloth around the edges to 1½ inches (3.8 cm) all around. Follow the steps on page 120 to hem the edges and finish your rug.

3

SARAPE RUG

Finished size: 30" × 20" (76.2 × 50.8 cm)

Sarapes are also known as the Mexican poncho. They are colorful, vibrant and recognizable. Sarapes are typically rectangular and woven with a stripe design. They have many different colors that complement each other, often forming a gradient from light to dark shades. This is my modern take on the sarape, a super fun piece that allows you to play with color like no other project.

BEFORE YOU START

If there was ever a project to use your leftover yarn stash, this is it! There is no limit to how many colors you can use or in what order. This is the best project to let loose and experiment. Because there are a lot of yarn changes, the project can take a little longer. A good tip is to punch as many sections with one color as you want before setting up for the next.

MATERIALS

- 30" × 20" (76.2 × 50.8 cm) monk's cloth, 13 thread count, plus enough to wrap around your frame (See the Stretcher Frames section, page 16.)
- Approximately 16 oz (454 g) total of wool yarn. I used many colors in different weights
- Yellow or cream-colored thread

TOOLS

- Sewing machine (optional)
- Fabric stretcher frame
- Size 10 regular Oxford punch needle
- Scissors
- Sewing needle
- Pins
- Iron
- Wet cloth

YARN COLORS

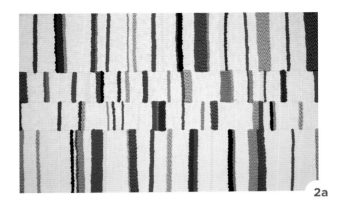
2a

2b

PUNCHING THE DESIGN

1. To prevent the monk's cloth from unraveling, zigzag the edges using a sewing machine and thread. If you don't have a sewing machine, you can skip this step.

    Stretch the monk's cloth tightly over your stretcher frame. Make sure it's taut and wrinkle-free.

    Divide your punching area into four sections: Measure and draw a stripe measuring 7 inches (17.8 cm) tall on the top and bottom of the canvas. The remaining middle stripe should be 6 inches (15.2 cm) tall; divide it in half to give you two stripes of 3 inches (7.6 cm) each. You should have a total of four horizontal stripes.

2. Start punching sections in different widths. Try to do as many as you can using the same color to avoid multiple yarn changes and save some time. Continue until all the rows are punched.

3. Once finished, trim any loose or long ends on the back and take your piece off the frame. Fix any large holes made by the frame on the monk's cloth around the edges using a needle or your punch tool.

    Trim the monk's cloth around the edges to 1½ inches (3.8 cm) all around. Follow the instructions on page 121 to finish the rug edges using the whipstitch binding method.

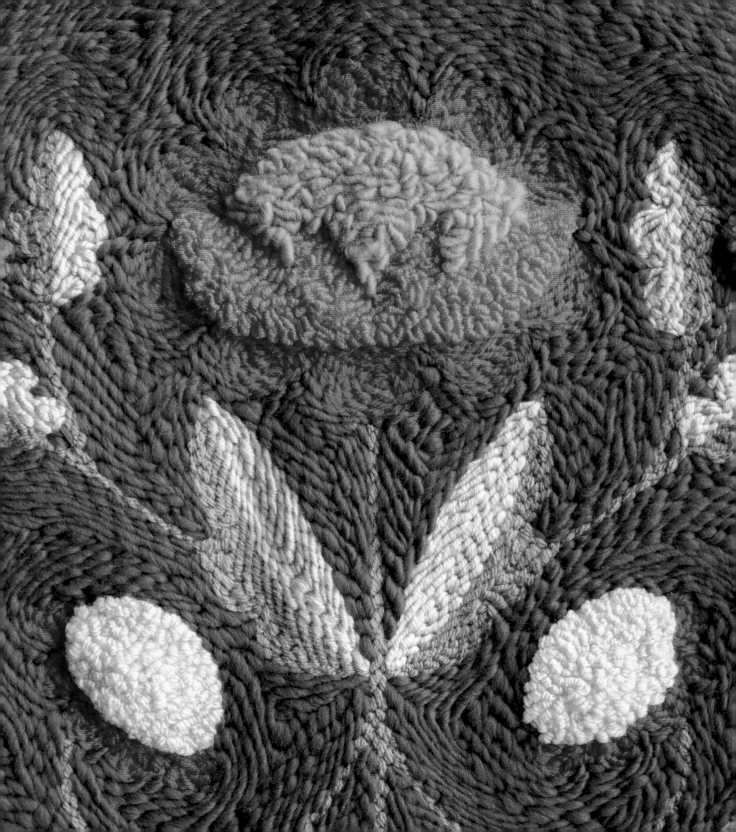

KITCHEN & DINING ACCESSORIES

Many of the crafts created by artisan women are for the kitchen. Today many of these crafts are used daily, which makes them an even more important part of everyday culture. I hope that some of the projects here will make it into your home.

Some yarns, such as cotton and wool, work well for handling hot surfaces; this makes them ideal for making mats or pot holders that will bring a fun element to your space. The smaller embroidery punch needle allows you to add a fun touch to other pieces such as napkins and aprons. Adding a small pop of color here and there makes a huge difference in the kitchen.

Most of Mexico's artisan crafts are made for daily use. They are created out of need and can be traced as far back as the Aztec era. Eventually, they became a staple in every household and today families take pride in cooking and serving secret family recipes in traditional cookware. Many of these were the inspiration for the patterns in this section. I hope that you will be inspired to make some for your kitchen.

CARPETA COASTERS

Finished size: 4¼" (10.8 cm) in diameter

Coasters are a fun project to brighten your table setting. This is a great first project to tackle if you're just getting comfortable with punch needle. The coasters are small, simple and quick to make. They are perfect for any leftover yarn you may have laying around, and they are a great hostess gift. Best of all, you can change them up as often as you'd like! This is your chance to use variegated yarns—sometimes bright or contrasting colors are all you need for a striking design. These coasters remind me of a miniature version of the straw table mats (carpetas) that are very popular in Mexican markets.

BEFORE YOU START

For this project you can make as few or as many coasters as you'd like—that's the beauty of it! Gather your yarn and feel free to wing a design instead of following my template, if you'd like. I used acrylic yarn for this as the process of blocking it with heat will make it fuse together, making a stronger coaster. Use the mini punch needle because you don't want the coaster to be too thick. You'll be using a whipstitch to finish the edges.

MATERIALS

- 14" × 14" (35.5 × 35.5 cm) of monk's cloth, 13 thread count
- Template
- Carbon paper
- Approximately 1 oz (28 g) of each color of medium-weight blue and yellow yarn (feel free to use your scraps)

TOOLS

- 12" (30.5-cm) no-slip Morgan embroidery hoop
- Compass
- Soft pencil
- Size 14 mini Oxford punch needle
- Scissors
- Iron
- Wet cloth
- Upholstery needle

YARN COLORS

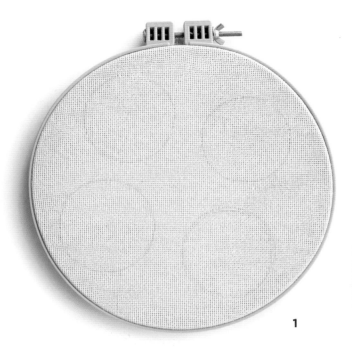

1

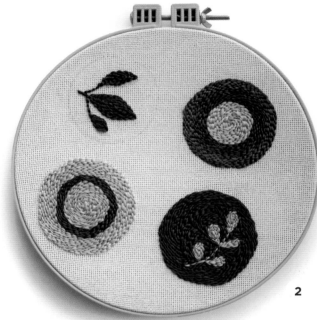

2

PUNCHING THE DESIGN

1. Stretch the monk's cloth on the embroidery hoop, making sure it's taut.

   With your compass draw four 4-inch (10-cm) circles, leaving about 1 inch (2.5 cm) in between them.

   Transfer the pattern by placing the carbon paper underneath the pattern template and tracing over it with a soft pencil. Be sure to apply constant pressure. Feel free to hand draw the motifs or make your own!

2. Start punching your designs. For the two coasters with concentric circles, start punching at the outer edge, working your way in. If you're punching motifs, punch those first before filling in the background.

3. When you're done punching, cut out each circle, leaving ½ inch (1.3 cm) all around and trim the loose strands on the back.

4. With the iron on the maximum heat setting, place the wet cloth on top of your coasters and press. Do not iron the coaster directly and be sure to apply constant pressure all around. Iron both sides, and within a few seconds you'll notice the loops and stitches begin to "melt" into each other.

   Trim any loose threads that may have come undone on the monk's cloth. Don't pull them! You want to keep the integrity of the weave as much as you can so that it stays together when you finish the edge. Follow the directions on page 121 for whipstitch binding to finish your coasters. Your coasters are ready to use!

3

4

PRIMOROSA TABLE NAPKIN

Finished size: 20″ × 20″ (50.8 × 50.8 cm)

When I came up with the pattern for this linen napkin, I knew it would lend itself well to the Ultra Punch needle. It's neutral enough to be incorporated into any color scheme. Making a whole set should be easy once you get the hang of the smaller punch needle. The design was inspired by a couple of barro negro pieces I brought back from my last trip in Mexico. These black clay pieces have very intricate and elaborate designs. The detailed openwork often features various patterns and floral motifs. This napkin's simplicity and elegance are the perfect addition to any table arrangement.

BEFORE YOU START

I used a 20″ × 20″ (50.8 × 50.8–cm) cotton-blend napkin for this that came in a pack of twelve. Feel free to make as many as you need to complete your table setting. I find that a monochromatic color scheme is easier to coordinate with, but feel free to use different colors if you'd like! For sealing the back, if you find your fabric adhesive too dry, stiff or rough, try using Cover-A-Stitch iron-on backing. You can find it at machine embroidery supply stores.

MATERIALS

- Template
- 20″ × 20″ (50.8 × 50.8–cm) cotton or linen napkin(s)
- Approximately 2 skeins per napkin of embroidery floss in black
- No-sew permanent fabric adhesive or Cover-A-Stitch™ Thermoseal

TOOLS

- Heat transfer pencil
- Iron
- 12″ (30.5-cm) no-slip Morgan embroidery hoop
- Ultra Punch punch needle tool with medium and large needles
- Scissors
- Stiff paintbrush (hog hair)

FLOSS COLORS

1

2

PUNCHING THE DESIGN

1. Transfer the pattern by drawing over the pattern with a heat transfer pencil. Trace the pattern from the back (against a window if necessary) or over top to have it be mirrored on your napkin. Place the pattern on top of your napkin and iron the pattern into place. Remember that the lines will be permanent so pay close attention to placement.

   Stretch the napkin on your hoop, making sure it's a snug fit.

   Punch using the needle set to the number 3 length. Using three strands of floss, outline the entire design. Punch two rows for each stem to get the desired thickness.

2. Flip the hoop so that you can punch the inside of the leaves and the flowers. Fill them all in.

3. Once you're done punching, apply the permanent fabric adhesive to the back using the stiff paintbrush. Your napkin is finished!

PEONÍA TABLE MAT

Finished size: 18″ (45.7 cm) in diameter

This peony circular—and symmetrical!—mat will add some brightness to your spread and protect your table. Use it as a centerpiece or as a heat-resistant surface. Be sure to only use cotton or wool yarn as these will not melt when they come in contact with heat. Using an extra layer of Insul-Fleece™ will make this extra heatproof! Feel free to modify this to make it as small or as big as you need it to be. This is a great versatile piece that you can also use as a pillow or as a seat cover on top of a bench or stool for added cushioning.

BEFORE YOU START

Because this mat will be getting lots of use and will be exposed to heat, I use a combination of cotton and wool yarn so that the yarn does not melt. If you'd like it to be extra heatproof add a layer of Insul-Fleece between the punched piece and the backing. Be sure to use a thinner yarn for the flower details, as the pattern lines can get quite thin in some areas. My binding edge is about 1 inch (2.5 cm) wide; you can go thinner if you'd like.

MATERIALS

- 16″ × 16″ (40.6 × 40.6 cm) monk's cloth, 13 thread count, plus enough to wrap around your frame (See the Stretcher Frames section, page 16.)
- Template
- Carbon paper
- Approximately 6½ oz (184 g) of medium-weight wool or cotton yarn in turquoise, 1 oz (28 g) each of yellow, light yellow, hot pink, coral, blue and light blue
- 17″ (43.2-cm)-diameter circle of canvas or heavyweight fabric
- One 17″ (43.2-cm)-diameter circle Insul-Fleece for heatproofing (optional)
- Matching thread

TOOLS

- Sewing machine (optional)
- Fabric stretcher frame
- Soft pencil
- Size 14 mini and size 10 fine or regular Oxford punch needle
- Wet cloth
- Iron
- Scissors
- Pins or sewing clips
- Upholstery needle

YARN COLORS

PUNCHING THE DESIGN

1. To prevent the monk's cloth from unraveling, zigzag the edges using a sewing machine and thread. This is optional but well worth it!

   Stretch the monk's cloth tightly over your stretcher frame. Make sure it's taut and wrinkle-free.

   Transfer the pattern by placing the carbon paper underneath the pattern template and tracing over it with a soft pencil. Be sure to apply constant pressure.

   Begin punching the leaves and stems with the blue and light blue yarn using the size 14 mini needle. Punch three rows for the longer stems and two rows for the stems with the coral balls.

   Tip: Remember to offset the stitches to get an even look.

2. With the light yellow yarn, outline the center of the bottom three flowers using the size 14 mini needle. Flip the piece to the back and punch the middle; this will give you the loops on the front. Continue with the darker yellow and the biggest flower.

3. Flip the piece. Using the hot pink yarn, punch the flower petals. For the biggest flower, outline the front two petals first with the coral yarn. Then punch on the reverse to get the loops on the front; this is the same process as the flower centers.

   Outline the flower buds (circles) with the coral, reverse and punch through the back using the size 10 needle.

4. It's time to finish the background. With the turquoise yarn and the size 14 mini needle, outline the floral motif and continue to punch the background through the front of the piece. Start by punching from the outer circle and outlining the flower motif. Once that's done, punch the rest of the gaps.

1

2

3

5

4

5. Once finished, take your piece off the frame. Place a wet cloth on top of your piece and using the highest setting on your iron, press. It should only take about 10 seconds per section. Once you see the cloth flattening out and relaxing a little, you'll know it's done.

   Cut off the excess monk's cloth leaving ½ inch (1.3 cm) around the perimeter. Place the heavyweight fabric underneath, wrong sides together; add the layer of Insul-Fleece in between, if you wish. Clip or pin together.

   Sew both pieces together using a straight stitch as close to the edge as possible.

   Follow the instructions for whipstitch binding on page 121 to finish the edge of your mat.

BLOOMING APRON

Mexican embroidered blouses were my inspiration for this project. They are known for their bright floral designs in different shapes and sizes that adorn primarily the neck and chest area. The Ultra Punch needle is the perfect tool for this project as the smaller stitches give you the freedom to play with color while getting an embroidered look that is perfect for embellishing this apron. For this project, you are welcome to flip and rotate the flowers however you like. Experiment with the different sizes or even hand draw them directly on the fabric using a water-soluble pen. Don't worry, you can always erase it if you don't like it.

BEFORE YOU START

This can be done on any material or style of apron—or even a shirt collar! I used two tones of floss for each of the flowers that show the loop on the front; this gives the flower more dimension. Look for colors that are two or three shades apart so that you can see the contrast. You can mix and match the colors according to the apron or even make all the flowers the same color. Because this piece will be washed, it's very important to seal the back to prevent the stitches from coming out in the wash. Using a no-sew permanent adhesive makes it safe for you to wash the garment following your apron's washing instructions.

MATERIALS

- Template
- Cotton or linen mix apron
- Approximately 1 skein of embroidery floss of each color in a variety of tones of pink, purple, coral, yellow and green
- No-sew permanent fabric adhesive

TOOLS

- Heat transfer pen
- Iron
- 12″ (30.5-cm) no-slip Morgan embroidery hoop
- Ultra Punch punch needle tool with medium needle
- Scissors
- Stiff paintbrush (hog hair)

FLOSS COLORS

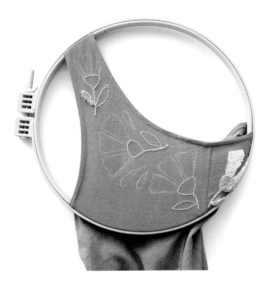

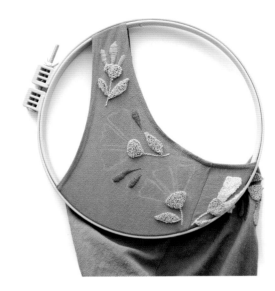

1

2

PUNCHING THE DESIGN

1. Transfer the pattern by drawing over it with a heat transfer pen. Place the pattern on top of one half of your apron and iron the pattern into place. Remember that the lines will be permanent, so pay close attention to placement. Now take the template, flip it over and trace it on the blank side. Trace the pattern (now inverted) with a heat transfer pencil. Place it on the other half of the apron and iron in place.

   Stretch the apron on your hoop, making sure it's a snug fit. I was able to fit half of the design, which is ideal to minimize the number of times you have to move your hoop.

   Start by outlining all the flower stems on the front. Use the medium needle set to number 3 in the length adjustment and three strands of floss. Punch two rows.

   Flip the hoop and punch from the back to fill in the shapes.

2. To punch the smaller flower and the tear-shaped leaves, change the needle length to number 5. Using the respective colors and three strands of floss, on the front of the hoop punch once on the edge of the shape and then another time on the opposite edge. Do this back and forth until you cover the whole shape, varying the length of the stiches to accommodate for the curved tip.

   As you are punching, it might be helpful to hold the floss loop underneath the hoop as you pull the needle to the other side. Floss can be slippery; it doesn't hurt to hold it in case you pull harder than you need to.

   Tip: If you find the threads to be loose, flip the hoop so you are looking at the back and pull the loops on both sides at the same time. This will tighten the stitch. Don't pull only one side as you will risk the other side coming undone.

3

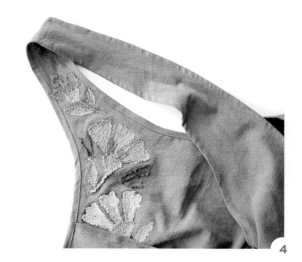

4

3. Finish the bigger flowers the same way you did the leaves. Change the needle length back to number 3. Outline the front of the petal using the dark shade at the bottom and the light shade at the top. Flip the hoop and continue punching from the back. You want the shades to blend in together; to do this punch vertical lines that vary in height that go up the middle of each petal. Once you're happy with the amount of stitches, change to the light color and fill in the rest of the petals.

4. Before you take the apron off the hoop and transfer to the opposite side, it's very important to seal the back. Apply the fabric adhesive using the stiff brush, making sure every stitch is covered. If your apron fabric is thin and somewhat see-through, brush the loops towards the inside of the shapes so that you don't get a shadow on the front. My apron is pretty thick and I didn't have this problem. I made sure to press the loops down so that I wouldn't have any stiff loops that could poke me or be uncomfortable when wearing the apron. Let it dry completely.

Transfer the hoop to the opposite side of the apron and repeat the above steps. You're done!

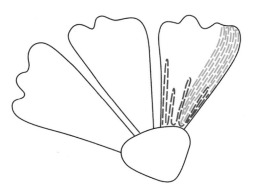

RETAMA HOT PADS

Finished size: 9" × 9" (23 × 23 cm)

Hot pads or pot holders are a staple in the kitchen—why not have some fun with them? This is a project where you can dip into your fabric stash. I used fabrics from my Amethyst Garden collection with Clothworks®. Feel free to mix and match any fabrics that you have available, but always use cotton. This is a great project to give as a hostess or Christmas gift; these are always handy to have around. The florals in these are inspired by a Veracruz traditional shawl or poncho that is worn in the Huasteca region. It depicts a rendition of a tiny and delicate flower called Retama by designer Ramón Valdiosera.

BEFORE YOU START

Make sure that the yarn you use is cotton or wool and that the fabric is 100% cotton or it will burn. You are welcome to make these smaller, but I find this size is more comfortable and big enough to grab hot stuff without fearing that I will burn my hands. These are also a great size to use under pots and pans if you don't have a heat-resistant surface. Feel free to make your own double-fold bias tape as I did!

MATERIALS

- 11" × 17" (28 × 43.2 cm) monk's cloth, 13 thread count, plus enough to wrap around your frame (See the Stretcher Frames section, page 16.)
- Template
- Carbon paper
- Approximately ½ oz (14 g) of each color of medium-weight wool or cotton yarn in white, pink, yellow, dark pink and speckled blue and 3 oz (85 g) of seafoam green
- 43" × 10" (109.2 × 25.4 cm) of cotton fabric
- 43" × 10" (109.2 × 25.4 cm) of Insul-Fleece
- 2½ yd (2.3 m) of ½" (1.3 cm)-wide double-fold bias tape
- Matching thread

TOOLS

- Sewing machine (optional)
- Fabric stretcher frame
- Soft pencil
- Size 14 mini Oxford punch needle
- Scissors
- Wet cloth
- Iron
- Pins or sewing clips

YARN COLORS

1

2

PUNCHING THE DESIGN

1. To prevent the monk's cloth from unraveling, zigzag the edges using a sewing machine and thread. This is optional but well worth it!

   Stretch the monk's cloth tightly over your stretcher frame. Make sure it's taut and wrinkle-free.

   Transfer the pattern by placing the carbon paper underneath the pattern template and tracing over it with a soft pencil. Be sure to apply constant pressure.

   Start by punching the flower alternating the white and pink petals and yellow center. Next, punch the leaves and the stems using the speckled blue.

2. Punch the remaining two flowers using the pink and dark pink followed by the rest of the background in seafoam green. Punch the corners square, rather than curved, following the template, as it gives you some room for error if the layers shift when you're sewing. You can also choose to round out the corners if it's easier for you.

   Tip: If you find that your yarn is too thick and think you might have an issue running it through your sewing machine, don't punch all the way to the edges of the template. Leave about ¼ inch (6.4 mm) of monk's cloth before you hit the edge of the template.

   Take your piece off the frame and trim any loose ends. Using the wet cloth, iron your piece using the highest setting. Press.

3

4

3. Cut all your pieces and layer them, putting the Insul-Fleece in the middle. Fabric and punched pieces should be facing out on both sides. Pin or clip them in place.

   Note: For the sides that had a punched piece, I only used one layer of Insul-Fleece as I felt it was enough; you are welcome to use two.

4. Stitch all around the four pieces using a straight stitch and a ⅛-inch (3.2-mm) seam allowance. Trim all sides and corners, making sure to remove any extra fabric to reduce bulk.

5. Time to assemble the hot pads. Layer the half pieces on top of the full pieces making sure the bottoms align. Baste the top corners on the half pieces so that they don't shift.

5

6

7

6. Unfold the bias tape and pin or clip it to the edge of the hot pad right sides together. I chose the back to be the side that doesn't have the punched piece. This seam will be covered once you flip over the bias tape. Sew in place leaving about a 2-inch (5-cm) gap before the ends meet.

7. Measure exactly where the ends meet and sew them together, right sides together to close the loop. Finish sewing the bias tape to the hot pad.

8. Once the back of the bias tape is attached, fold it and flip it towards the front going over all the layers. The raw edge of the pad should be sandwiched in between the two sides of the bias tape. Sew all the way around. Your hot pads are ready to use!

8

SEATING,
STORAGE & MORE

Sometimes you need to spice up a little corner in your entryway or a nook in your living room. The beauty of punch needle is that you can practically make it into anything you want. I often find myself walking around my house looking for an object I can add a touch of punch needle to—it's seriously addicting. To me, it's a huge bonus when a piece serves a practical purpose! One of my favorites is the Otomí Storage Cushion (page 97) because it's a storage solution and a great conversation piece!

As with any of the projects that you see in this book, I encourage you to see beyond the object and change it up. If you like a particular pillow pattern but you don't want a pillow, feel free to make it into something else. Anything goes in your home! There's nothing better than coming home to a place that inspires you. This section will give you some project ideas to spruce up a room or section of your home that will make it feel your own.

OTOMÍ STORAGE CUSHION

Finished size: 18″ × 18″ (45.7 × 45.7 cm)

One of the best parts of punch needle is that you can apply it to almost anything. I love when a piece I'm creating serves a purpose. This project is a hiding spot while also serving as a floor cushion and a colorful statement piece in your home. I found that it's the perfect solution for storing that large blanket that you don't necessarily want lying around the living room all day long. I also thought it was the perfect size to incorporate a design inspired by Otomí embroidery. Also known as the Tenango style, it originates in the state of Hidalgo in the municipality of Tenango de Doria. This technique became the main source of income for the women of the region in 1960 when the area was affected by a drought. One of the most recognized characteristics of this type of embroidery is the use of color. Otomí pieces use a variety of bright colors that depict iconic and stylized imagery of local animals and plants. While found mostly on white or cream-colored fabric, some Otomí pieces use black as a contrasting background. You can choose to use whichever one you like; I chose black as it will hide dirt better on this floor piece.

BEFORE YOU START

You are welcome to modify this cushion to whatever fits your needs best. Adding a zipper is a great idea. There are also many ways to stuff it: you can use new or recycled upholstery foam or even old clothes that you plan to donate. Feel free to experiment to get the firmness you want. Because it will be getting lots of use, reach for the wool yarns. If your fabric is not heavy or stiff enough to hold the shape of the cushion, use interfacing fabric to stiffen it up.

MATERIALS

- 18″ × 18″ (45.7 × 45.7 cm) monk's cloth, 13 thread count, plus enough to wrap around your frame (See the Stretcher Frames section, page 16.)
- Template
- Carbon paper
- Approximately 7½ oz (213 g) of medium-weight or lightweight wool yarn in black, and less than ½ oz each of light and dark purple, light and dark green, light and dark blue, white, yellow, orange, mauve, red, pink and hot pink
- Interfacing for your fabric if it's not thick enough (the same amount as the heavy-duty fabric; optional)
- 2 (19″ × 14″ [48.3 × 35.5-cm]) pieces of black, thick, heavy-duty fabric
- 4 (19″ × 8″ [48.3 × 20.3-cm]) pieces of black, thick, heavy-duty fabric
- Matching thread

TOOLS

- Sewing machine (optional)
- Fabric stretcher frame
- Soft pencil
- Size 14 mini and size 10 fine or regular Oxford punch needle
- Scissors
- Wet cloth
- Iron
- Pins or sewing clips

YARN COLORS

1a

1b

PUNCHING THE DESIGN

1. To prevent the monk's cloth from unraveling, zigzag the edges using a sewing machine and thread. This optional step is well worth it!

    Stretch the monk's cloth tightly over your stretcher frame. Make sure it's taut and wrinkle-free.

    Transfer the pattern by placing the carbon paper underneath the pattern template and tracing over it with a soft pencil. Be sure to apply constant pressure.

Using the needle that fits your yarn, begin punching the design. You can start with any shape you want. To make things go a little faster, try punching the same-colored shapes to avoid rethreading the needle.

Once the design is completely punched, begin punching the background using the black yarn.

2

3

2. Once it's finished, take your piece off the frame and trim any loose ends. Using the wet cloth, iron your piece using the highest setting. Press.

   Trim the monk's cloth around your piece to ½ inch (1.3 cm) all around. You should have a piece that is 19 × 19 inches (48.3 × 48.3 cm).

3. If you want to use interfacing to make your cushion even more study, apply it now to the sides and bottom pieces.

   Take the 2 (19 × 14–inch [48.3 × 35.5–cm]) large pieces of heavy-duty fabric and fold over about ¼ inch (6.4 mm) from the longest edge (wrong sides together) and press. Fold a second time and press. Sew the hem on each piece using a straight stitch just like you would if you were making an envelope pillow (page 122).

   Lay them on top of each other, right sides facing down, to make a 19 × 19–inch (48.3 × 48.3–cm) square that will be the bottom of your cushion. Pin the overlapping parts and baste them together so they don't shift.

4

4. Pin the small rectangle pieces to each side of your punched piece, right sides together. Using a straight stitch and a ½-inch (1.3-cm) seam, sew all the pieces in place.

   Tip: Sew with the punched piece facing up so that you can make sure no monk's cloth is showing.

   Attach the envelope back to the bottom short side with right sides together.

5. Next, start giving shape to your cushion by assembling the cube. Start by sewing together the smaller sides around the punched piece and then the envelope back. Clip all the corners and sides in place and start sewing all the seams together. Pay attention to the corners to make sure they are sewn properly. Clip them carefully to reduce bulk before you turn the cushion right side out.

   Tip: Zigzag the edges to prevent the fabric from fraying.

   Turn the cushion right side out and stuff. You're done!

5

MONO STOOL

Finished size: 10" × 10" (25.4 × 25.4 cm)

I associate Mexican embroidery with a black background. It helps bright flowers stand out and the piece instantly gets a more refined, elegant look. Having a dark background on a stool also hides any dirt that it will inevitably accumulate and makes the design pop. I find having a stool around the house super handy, especially with young children. You never know what you'll need to reach! If you're wondering what mono means, it's a way of saying cute in Spanish. This little stool is decorative and functional, perfect for leaving out when it's not needed.

BEFORE YOU START

This pattern can be easily adapted to any size stool. Be sure to measure your surface to determine how much monk's cloth you'll need. I also added a 1¼-inch (3.2-cm) lip to the design so that it could wrap around the sides; this will prevent the monk's cloth from showing. I stapled the cover on the stool; you can choose to sew corner ties or elastic onto it to make it removable.

MATERIALS

- 10" × 10" (25.4 × 25.4 cm) monk's cloth (or more), 13 thread count, plus enough to wrap around your stool and your frame (See the Stretcher Frames section, page 16.)
- Template
- Carbon paper
- Approximately 3 oz (85 g) of medium-weight wool yarn in black, ½ oz (14 g) of each color of medium-weight wool in variegated red, pink, green, dark green, turquoise and yellow
- Square stool

TOOLS

- Sewing machine (optional)
- Fabric stretcher frame
- Soft pencil
- Size 14 mini or size 10 fine or regular Oxford punch needle
- Scissors
- Staple gun

YARN COLORS

1

2

PUNCHING THE DESIGN

1. To prevent the monk's cloth from unraveling, zigzag the edges using a sewing machine and thread. If you don't have a sewing machine, you can skip this step.

   Stretch the monk's cloth tightly over your stretcher frame. Make sure it's taut and wrinkle-free.

   If possible, trace the contour of your stool so you have the right size for your pattern.

   Transfer the pattern by placing the carbon paper underneath the pattern template and tracing over it with a soft pencil. Be sure to apply constant pressure.

   Outline the flower petals with the black yarn on all the flowers. Punch the petals alternating between the variegated red and pink yarns for some contrast. Punch the yellow centers.

2. Punch the leaves and stems using turquoise and the two shades of green.

3. Punch the background using the black yarn. After measuring the side (lip) of your stool, punch around the design adding the extra height that you need to wrap it around. This will prevent the monk's cloth from showing on the sides. You can use any color you'd like.

   Take your piece off the frame. Trim around it, leaving half an inch (1.3 cm) of monk's cloth. Zigzag the edges with a sewing machine and staple to your stool. It's finished!

3

MARGARITA LAMPSHADE

Finished size: 8½" (20.3 cm) in diameter

I find lamps very hard to fit in with the rest of my décor, especially because they can be expensive with not a lot of choices to choose from. If you've invested in a lamp that no longer works for your space, changing up the shade is a great DIY project to tackle. I opted for a neutral color scheme, but feel free to change it up to suit your space. The simple yet elegant floral motif gives the lamp a whole new look!

BEFORE YOU START

This is a good project to give an old lamp a makeover. I used different shades of the colors to create a gradient effect; this is of course optional and can work with any shades. I didn't follow a specific order for the flower so feel free to combine colors to your liking!

MATERIALS

- Template
- 29" × 11" (73.7 × 27.9 cm) natural linen fabric, dimensions might vary depending on your lampshade
- 1 skein of embroidery floss of each color in a variety of tones of yellow, green and brown
- No-sew permanent fabric adhesive
- 8½" (20.3-cm) lampshade

TOOLS

- Heat transfer pen
- 12" (30.5-cm) no-slip Morgan embroidery hoop
- Ultra Punch punch needle tool with medium needle
- Stiff paintbrush (hog hair)
- Iron
- Wet cloth
- Scissors
- Spray adhesive

FLOSS COLORS

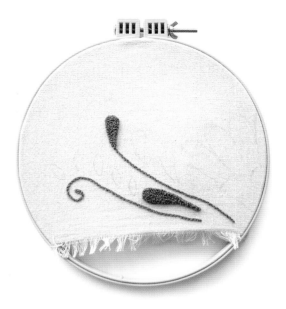

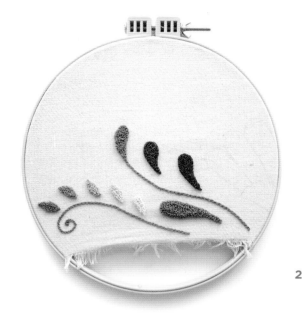

1

2

PUNCHING THE DESIGN

1. Transfer the pattern by drawing over the pattern with a heat transfer pen. Place the pattern on top of your linen and iron the pattern into place. Remember that the lines will be permanent, so pay close attention to placement. This is a good project to try tracing the pattern against the light.

   I chose to fray the bottom of the linen. This is optional, but I did this before I placed it on the hoop. Stretch the linen on your hoop making sure it's a snug fit.

   Punch the biggest leaf and stems using the light green. Use the needle set to the number 3 length and use three strands of floss. I outlined the leaf shape first and punched two rows for each of the stems. To fill in the leaves, I flipped the hoop and punched from the back.

2. Continue outlining the rest of the leaves with different shades of brown and green. Then flip and punch from the back to fill them in.

   Using the stiff brush, apply the permanent fabric adhesive to the back to secure the stitches. Be sure to brush them inwards so that you don't get a shadow on the outside of the leaves when the light is turned on. Let it dry completely before taking it off the hoop.

   Tip: Press down the floss so that you don't end up with a bumpy back once it's dry. Bumps will make it harder to glue to the shade.

   Once the adhesive is dry, take the piece off the hoop and center it on the opposite side. Repeat the same steps, making sure it's a mirror image. Apply adhesive to the back and let it dry completely.

3

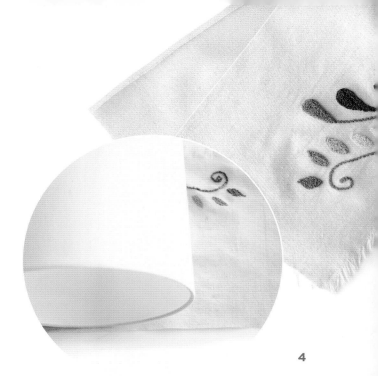

4

3. Once both sides are completed, center the hoop on the middle flower. Using the light green, outline the bottom of the flower, then reverse the hoop and punch from the back to fill it in.

   The next step is to fill in the petals: Switch the needle length to number 5. Insert the needle on one side, then pull it over and insert it on the other side. Go back and forth, following the curvature at the top making the stitches shorter each time. Continue with all the petals, using different colors for each.

   Tip: Hold the loop on the bottom with one finger as you pull the needle so that the stitch doesn't come out.

   Brush the adhesive on the back to seal the stitches and let it dry completely. Take the piece off the hoop and iron any wrinkles out.

   Note: To smooth out wrinkles in between the punched flowers, apply a wet cloth on top and iron it using a low heat setting.

4. Place the linen against the lamp shade and measure once more. In order to get a clean edge, I measured ¼ inch (6.4 mm) above the lip of the shade and cut off the rest. Do the same for the vertical seam, making sure the linen wraps around the shade completely. Fold over that excess fabric on the top and side and press down.

   Glue down that lip using permanent fabric adhesive. Let it dry completely.

   The final step is to glue the linen onto the shade: Spray the back of the linen with the spray adhesive and carefully align it to the shade. Roll the linen on carefully while keeping it taut to avoid wrinkles. Your lampshade is done!

MOSAIC STORAGE BIN

Finished size: 18″ × 18″ (45.7 × 45.7 cm)

Mexican textiles often incorporate colorful symmetrical patterns featuring squares or rectangles. This type of pattern is really easy to get excited about; it can be made as complicated or as simple as you want. Focus on bright color combinations. This is your chance to play with color and perhaps use leftover yarn that you have around the house! A muted monochromatic combination of colors would also suit a quieter décor style.

BEFORE YOU START

Scope out the piece you'd like to cover. Vintage or forgotten items work great for this project, so look around to see what you can find. I chose an old storage bin that needed some love. Other options are a stool, a seat cushion or even a headboard. It's a good idea to cut out a couple of different size squares to place on the piece you plan to cover to get an idea of scale; smaller squares work best for a small piece. You want to fit a good number of squares on your piece to get more color in. This is also a great project to use leftover or scrap pieces of yarn. This pattern is easy to modify to suit any shape. Feel free to add or remove blocks to suit your piece. A fine punch needle works best with linen.

MATERIALS

- 18″ × 18″ (45.7 × 45.7 cm) natural linen fabric, plus enough to wrap around your frame (See the Stretcher Frames section, page 16. Be sure to measure the piece you need to cover for exact measurements.)
- Approximately 1 oz (28 g) of each color of medium-weight wool yarn in hot pink, light pink, yellow, teal, purple, white and coral
- A storage bin with a lid. A removable lid makes it easier.

TOOLS

- Fabric stretcher frame
- Water-soluble transfer pen
- Ruler
- Scrap paper
- Scissors
- Size 14 mini Oxford punch needle
- Spray bottle
- Wet cloth
- Iron
- Stapling gun

YARN COLORS

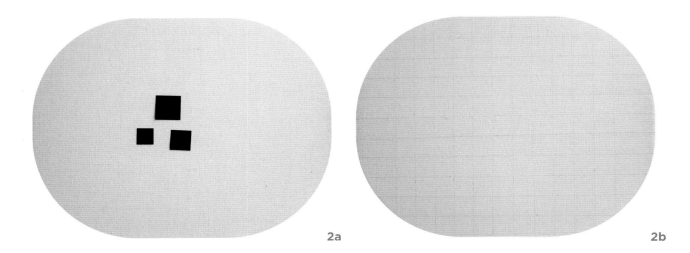

2a

2b

PUNCHING THE DESIGN

1. Measure the piece of furniture you want to cover. Get the right amount of fabric and a large enough frame. Then stretch the linen tightly over your stretcher frame. Make sure it's taut and wrinkle-free.

   Using the water-soluble transfer pen, trace or draw the shape of your piece on your fabric.

2. Use the ruler to draw two or three different sized squares on a scrap piece of paper. Cut them out and place them on your fabric to get an idea of what scale works best for the size of your piece. I used 1¼-inch (3.2-cm) squares for my grid.

Measure and draw your grid using the water-soluble pen.

Note: Be sure to center your middle square; you can use your cutout to eyeball the center and draw from there. This diamond design looks best when it's centered.

3. Start by punching the light pink cross in the middle. Continue punching the outer squares with white, yellow and hot pink.

4. Next, to get the triangle shapes punch half of a square by cutting across in a diagonal in purple and the other half in teal.

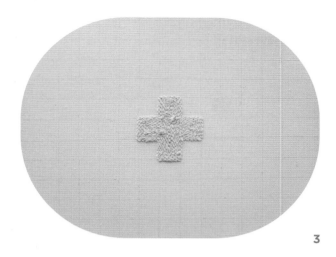

3

4

5. If you have any gaps you'd like to fill around the shape of your piece, add full or half squares around the design. Feel free to experiment!

Once you're done punching, take your spray bottle and wet the linen slightly to take off the transfer pen. You don't need very much at all. Rub carefully with your fingers. Take your piece off the frame.

Take a wet cloth and place it on top of your piece. Iron it on a hot setting.

Once your piece is set and wrinkle-free, wrap it around the lip of your furniture piece. Staple it in place. You're done!

5

BARRO PLANT POT

Finished size: 7" (17.8 cm) tall

The Mexican clay "olla" or cooking pot is a traditional staple in the kitchen. I have many fond memories of my grandparents cooking delicious meals in these pots. The clay enhances the flavors every time it's used, making it the go-to for every meal. The pots are hand-painted with simple designs that use few colors. Flowers and dotted patterns are seen on most traditional pots; they are unique and recognizable in every Mexican kitchen. The terracotta color is a warm brown-orange tone that brings warmth to any home. For this project, the flower motif can be easily duplicated to make a bigger plant pot.

BEFORE YOU START

If you have a specific pot in mind that you'd like to slip into this punched piece, be sure to measure its diameter and resize as needed. Remember to always use a liner at the bottom to prevent damage between waterings. It can be tricky working with smaller shapes; if not punched correctly the shapes will merge into each other forming a big blob. To avoid this, I like to outline them with the background yarn first and then fill them in. This ensures that there's enough space between them to see each shape individually. Use a fine punch needle and medium-weight yarn for this project since the spacing between leaves can get quite narrow.

MATERIALS

- 18" × 9" (45.7 × 23 cm) monk's cloth, 13 thread count, plus enough to wrap around your frame (See Stretcher Frames section on page 16.)
- Template
- Carbon paper
- Approximately 1 oz (28 g) of each color of medium-weight wool yarn in speckled black, white and yellow and 4 oz (113 g) of terracotta brown yarn
- Black thread
- 6½" (16.5-cm) circle of black canvas fabric

TOOLS

- Sewing machine (optional)
- Fabric stretcher frame
- Ruler
- Soft pencil
- Size 14 mini and size 10 fine Oxford punch needle
- Scissors
- Iron
- Wet cloth
- Sewing clips or pins

YARN COLORS

PUNCHING THE DESIGN

1. To prevent the monk's cloth from unraveling, zigzag the edges using a sewing machine and thread. This is optional but well worth it!

   Stretch the monk's cloth tightly over your stretcher frame. Make sure it's taut and wrinkle-free.

   Measure an 18 × 7¾-inch (45.7 × 23-cm) rectangle and punch the outline with the terracotta brown yarn.

   Transfer the pattern twice. Place it side by side; you can even flip one upside down to create some interest. Remember to leave at least 1½ inches (3.8 cm) from the top edge as this will be folded down to make the rim once the piece is finished. Transfer it by placing the carbon paper underneath the pattern template and tracing over it with a soft pencil. Be sure to apply constant pressure.

2. With the terracotta brown yarn and the size 14 mini needle, outline the leaves around the flowers first. Punch just outside the transfer line to ensure you keep the shapes the same size.

   Next, outline the inside of the shapes you just punched with the black yarn.

   To give some height to the black leaves flip the frame and punch from the back.

3. Next, punch the center of the flower with yellow yarn using a size 10 fine needle from the back of the piece.

   Punch the flower using white yarn.

   Repeat the same steps for the second half of the piece.

4. Punch the background using the terracotta brown yarn.

1

2

3

4

Punch a 1½-inch (3.8-cm) strip of yellow on the top edge of your piece. This will make the rim of the pot.

5. Take your piece off the frame and trim the monk's cloth to about ½ inch (1.3 cm) all around. Zigzag the edges.

    Using a damp cloth, iron your piece at a high temperature to flatten it out. Roll the yellow edge once to tuck in the monk's cloth and again to position it as the rim of your pot. Press in place.

    Optional: You can sew down the edge by hand using the technique I used to finish the floor mat on page 120.

6. Fold the piece in half, right sides together and sew the edges using a straight stitch. Be sure to sew over your punched stitches to ensure the monk's cloth doesn't show. Zigzag the edge.

7. Using sewing clips, clip the black canvas fabric to the bottom edge of your piece.

    Sew all around making sure you are sewing on top of your punched stitches so that no monk's fabric will show once it's turned. Trim the excess fabric and zigzag or sew to prevent unraveling.

    Turn your pot right side out, insert a potted plant and it's finished!

FINISHING TECHNIQUES

For any kind of finishing you choose to do, it's important to prep your piece for the final touches. Trim any loose ends and long loops. Then iron your piece: Use the hot/high temperature setting. Take a wet—not dripping—cloth and place it on top of the loop side. Iron it, applying slight pressure. This will flatten your piece and take care of any uneven loops.

Here are some of the ways I finish the projects in this book.

HEMMING THE EDGES

Hemming the edges is a way to prevent the monk's cloth from unraveling. It gives a nice clean finish to your piece. Follow these steps:

1. Fold in each corner and press. Feel free to use the same damp towel or a thinner cloth on top. You can trim any excess fabric so that the tip is tucked in once you fold in the rest of the sides.

2. Fold in each side of the rug and press.

3. Once the sides are folded in, fold each side once more so that the raw edges are hidden. Press.

4. Pin the folds so that the corners meet up and the sides are flat.

   Starting at one of the corners, thread the needle through the tip of the corner and sew the seam shut using a ladder stitch. This will make for invisible stitches. You can also use a whipstitch, if you prefer.

5. Continue sewing the sides by inserting the needle through the punched yarn and monk's cloth, and back up through the folded monk's cloth. Come out about one or two squares (0.5 cm) from the edge.

6. Continue sewing all around leaving about ¼ inch (6.4 mm) between stitches. Your piece is finished!

WHIPSTITCH BINDING

A whipstitch is a common and simple stitch that is done by hand. It wraps yarn around the edge of the monk's cloth; this hides the edge and prevents it from unraveling. It also gives your piece a thicker and finished edge. It is easier to bind if you leave enough monk's cloth to fold in as you sew. For a whipstitch binding, follow these steps:

1. Thread an upholstery needle with a double strand of yarn. Looking at the front of your piece, insert the needle just above the last punched row. Leave a ¾-inch (2-cm) tail. Re-insert the needle from the back passing right beside the first stitch and repeat making sure the tail is tucked inside the loops. Always pull softly and not too tight. Make the loops the same size as your cloth edge.

    Tip: If you find the monk's cloth is unraveling, carefully push each strand in the opposite direction and tuck them under your yarn as you are sewing. This will prevent them from sticking up. Be sure to always have both of your yarn strands side by side and not twisted!

2. If you run out of yarn, thread the needle back through the loops so that it's hidden. Trim. Re-thread the needle and repeat the process until you're finished.

    When you've finished the edge, cover with a wet cloth or towel and press with a hot iron. You're done!

1

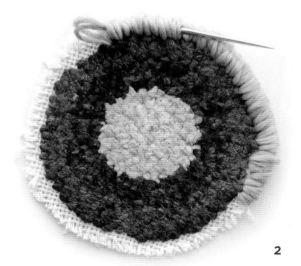

2

1 **2** **3**

MAKING THE ENVELOPE PILLOW COVER

To make a pillow cover for the projects in this book (pages 51, 55 and 59) or for one you design yourself, follow these steps:

1. Take your backing pieces and fold over about ¼ inch (6.4 mm) from the longest edge (wrong sides together) and press. Fold a second time and press. Sew the hem on each piece using a straight stitch. Lay your punched piece right side facing up (see photo) and your backing pieces overlapping on top, right sides facing down. The opening should be in the middle of the pillow cover.

   Pin all the way around the pillow cover to prevent the pieces from moving as you sew them to your punched piece.

2. Sew all four sides using a ¼-inch (6.4-mm) seam allowance. You want to place the needle as close as you can to the edge. Use the punched side facing up as a guide to make sure you are right on edge. This will prevent the monk's cloth showing once it's turned.

3. Trim the corners to avoid bulk when it's turned. Be careful not to cut the stitching. Trim any excess fabric around the perimeter of the pillow.

   Turn right side out and insert your pillow form. You're done!

SEALING THE BACK

When working with the Ultra Punch needle, it is almost always necessary to seal the back to prevent the stitches from coming out. Because the floss is thin and slippery, it's easier to accidentally pull it out when the piece is handled. To seal your project, follow these steps:

1. Place glue on the stitches on the back. Be generous, you want them to be completely coated.

2. Use a stiff brush to disperse the glue, making sure every stitch is coated. Brush the loops inwards so that they rest inside the shape that was punched; if you don't, you will get a shadow on the front around what was punched.

Let your piece dry completely overnight. Your work is now sealed!

MATERIALS SOURCE LIST

Here is a list of places to find punch needle materials. Most of these stores will have everything you need.

USA

amyoxford.com – Amy is the inventor of the Oxford punch needle and offers a variety of materials and online tutorials
amazon.com
etsy.com
hobbylobby.com
joann.com
michaels.com
nistockfarms.com
sealharborrug.com
woolandthegang.com
woolery.com

CANADA

redmapleruggery.ca
rugkit.co.uk
theknitcafetoronto.com
theworkroom.ca

ABROAD

etsy.com/shop/threelittleloops
studio-koekoek.com

ACKNOWLEDGMENTS

As always, it couldn't have been done without the support of my husband and my immediate family who allowed me the time to work on this throughout the summer. Writing two books back-to-back is no easy task!

Special thanks to my parents who encouraged me to explore my roots and culture through punch needle, and my mom who traveled with me to Mexico to learn and be inspired once more. Visiting local artisans was the highlight of our trip.

Rose Pearlman, I'll never forget your sweet words of reassurance and optimism when I began this journey. As an experienced fiber artist and rug hooker, your words meant a lot to me. To my friend Carlos Medina, for his constant support and encouragement and for being my sounding board, thank you! Lorrie and Donna, thank you so much for letting me come to your beautiful house to shoot some of the photos. Lastly, to Amy Oxford for her support and all she's done for the rug hooking community. Truly admirable.

Thank you once more to Page Street Publishing for encouraging me to write a punch needle book and for trusting me to write it before my first one was out into the world. The support and encouragement I received was truly appreciated! Thank you Rebecca Fofonoff for being my editor once more.

ABOUT THE AUTHOR

Melissa is a graphic designer, illustrator and event planner who is passionate about all things handmade. She is originally from Monterrey, Mexico, and is deeply influenced by its rich culture and history. She currently lives in Milton, Ontario, with her husband, Tom, twin boys, Wesley and Elliott, and two cats, Milo and Benjamin.

Always having a passion for the visual arts, Melissa received an honors bachelor's degree in graphic design from the joint program at York University and Sheridan College. She pursued her passion for handmade crafts with her first business Milo&Ben, creating sewn and needle-felted animals based on her illustrations. After winding down Milo&Ben, Melissa went on to write her first book, *Handmade Animal Dolls*, a how-to book on how to make her stuffed animals.

You can find her and her current projects on Instagram @melissalowrydesign. Please tag her and @vibrantpunchneedle during your punching journey!

INDEX